*Pillow*POP

25 QUICK-SEW PROJECTS TO BRIGHTEN YOUR SPACE

COMPILED BY HEATHER BOSTIC

Text, Photography, and Artwork copyright © 2013 by C&T Publishing, Inc.

Publisher: Amy Marson

Creative Director: Gailen Runge

Art Director/Book Designer: Kristy Zacharias

Editors: Phyllis Elving and Cynthia Bix

Technical Editors: Sadhana Wray and Gailen Runge

Page Layout Artist: Kerry Graham

Production Coordinator: Jessica Jenkins

Production Editor: S. Michele Fry

Illustrator: Tim Manibusan

Styled Photography by Christina Straw Photography

Pillow Photography by Diane Pedersen of C&T Publishing, Inc.

Photography Assistant: Cara Prado

Published by Stash Books, an imprint of C&T Publishing, Inc., P.O. Box 1456, Lafayette, CA 94549

Library of Congress Cataloging-in-Publication Data

Bostic, Heather, editor of compilation.

Pillow pop : 25 quick-sew projects to brighten your space / complied by Heather Bostic.

pages cm

ISBN 978-1-60705-478-8 (soft cover)

1. Pillows. 2. Patchwork--Patterns. I. Title.

TT410.B67 2013

746.46--dc23

5153 6612 3/13

2012026277

Printed in China

10 9 8 7 6 5 4 3 2 1

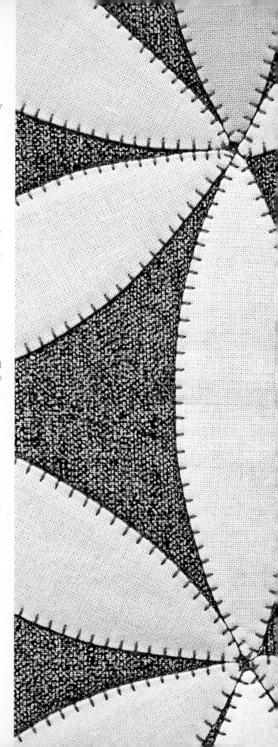

contents

Acknowledgments

It is my honor to thank my talented contributors for their outstanding designs and true friendships. This book is a testament to an idea that led me and my friend Kerri Horsley to create The Pillow Talk {Swap} on Flickr. Strangers came together with the concept of swapping pillows made from modern designs. Finding that strong commonality led to new relationships that will far outlive any terrific cushion—though the cushions are the sparkle of the endeavor.

Through this process, two companies have stood behind this book in an immeasurable way. So I'd like to humbly thank Stash Books for believing in me, this book, and my friends' designs. Also my sincere gratitude goes to Robert Kaufman Fabrics for its willing support of designers, and to Allie Heath personally for always providing fabrics with excitement and integrity. Thank you!

And last, I must give a huge thank-you to my ladies—my grandmother, Margaret A. Dean, for giving me the artist's curiosity and itch to create, and my Sweet Hot Yams for their relentless support of everything I attempt. You women mean the world to me.

X, Heather

Who Is Heather?

Heather Bostic ({House} of A La Mode) lives in beautiful Portland, Oregon. She's a wife, a stay-at-home mother of two beautiful boys, and an autism activist. Sewing was an easy choice for relaxation while raising a child with autism, although … what started out as a hobby for her has turned into a manic compulsion that has an appetite of its very own. She just can't help herself! Combine that with her Flickr site, her blog life, and the new Sewing Lounge/Studio in her hometown, and you have one serious nonstop party!

Heather tries to bring a masculine feel to her designs regardless of the fabrics being used, to create an edgy, urban look that she embraces as her true style. She credits the men in her life as her main source of inspiration for finding her rhythm—her amazing husband, Aaron; her two wonderful sons, Reed and Colin; and her father, Michael. She says they have been her biggest fans and supporters.

INTRODUCTION

Hello, friends! And welcome to my manic need to have sensational "statement pieces" as home decor pillows. There is simply nothing that snatches people's attention more when entering a space than a fabulous throw pillow!

A pillow could be a purely functional object, but you can elevate the commonplace cushion into something unique by making it a design statement. Design typically happens when you make a detailed drawing, deciding on the look and function of something (a building, a garment, or some other object). This act produces functional art—art that embraces our personal tastes and thus exhibits our styles to the world.

Whether you use this book as an inspiration tool, as a skill builder, or even as a beginning reference for quilting techniques, you'll find a wealth of ideas to keep you moving. You'll be empowered to walk away from mass-produced retail products and to let your own beautiful, artistic voice be heard!

You will find many techniques to try in the following pages, from appliqué to foundation piecing to quilting. Play around with color and texture in the patterns you select. And remember to have *fun* making these functional statement pieces that will bring a punch of design to your space!

X, Heather

Introduction

FAIR FEATHERED FRIENDS

Finished size: 20″ × 20″   *Quilted by Angela Walters*

Have you ever had any houseguests that you considered a little bit ... er ... bird-brained? Give your visitors—winged or not—a comfy place to sit by adding these versatile pillows to your chairs and couches. This beginner-friendly pattern is a great way to highlight various prints from the same fabric line or to use up your leftover pieces from other projects for a scrappier look.

Directional prints are great for this pillow—and if you rotate the prints on four different pillow tops, you can easily come up with four different looks.

Materials and Supplies

PRINT AND SOLIDS: coordinating scraps totaling ½ yard* for pillow top

MUSLIN OR OTHER LIGHTWEIGHT FABRIC: 22″ × 22″ for pillow top lining

BACKING: ½ yard of 42″ fabric

BATTING: 22″ × 22″

PILLOW FORM: 20″ square

* I used 11 different fabrics for a scrappy look, including fabrics from Laurie Wisbrun's "Nesting Chairs" and shot cottons, which use different colors for the warp (lengthwise) and weft (crosswise) threads, adding great depth and texture to modern designs.

ARTIST: *John Q. Adams*
WEBSITE: quiltdad.com

John is a husband and a father of three, who enjoys sewing and quilting in his spare time. Inspired by crafting blogs and vibrant, modern quilting fabrics, in 2004 John convinced his wife, Kiely, to teach him how to use a sewing machine. He started his popular blog "Quilt Dad" in 2008. John designs quilt patterns for both fabric designers and companies and contributes frequently to blogs, books, and other collaborative endeavors. He is a co-founder of the e-zine *Fat Quarterly*.

Born and raised in Brooklyn, New York, John lives in Holly Springs, North Carolina, with his wife; twin daughters, Megan and Bevin; and son, Sean. He earned his undergraduate and master's degrees at the University of North Carolina at Chapel Hill and, when not sewing, enjoys cheering for the Tar Heels.

Cutting

BACKING FABRIC: Cut 2 pieces 14˝ × 20½˝.

FABRIC SCRAPS: Cut pieces using sizes given in the pillow top assembly diagram.

tip *You can cut all the pieces up front, but I recommend you select fabrics along the way and cut as you go. If you use directional prints, be aware of their orientation as you cut and sew.*

INSTRUCTIONS

All seam allowances are ¼˝ unless otherwise indicated.

Making the Pillow Top

1. This pillow top is sewn in rows. For row 1, sew a 2½˝ × 8½˝ rectangle to a 2½˝ × 12½˝ rectangle. Press seams as you prefer, either open or to the side.

2. For row 2, sew a 1½˝ × 14½˝ rectangle to a 1½˝ × 6½˝ rectangle. Press.

3. Sew row 1 to row 2 to create a section 3½˝ × 20½˝.

4. Continue for rows 3 through 11, adding each completed row to the pillow top as you go. The pillow top should measure 20½˝ × 20½˝.

5. Layer muslin lining, batting, and the completed pillow top; baste. Quilt as desired. Trim all layers to 20½˝ × 20½˝.

Finishing

Refer to Pillow Construction Techniques (page 116) to make an envelope backing. The backing pieces will overlap by about 8˝. Sew the backing to the pillow top using a ¼˝ seam.

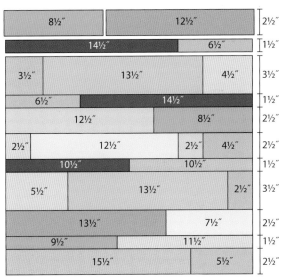

Assembly diagram

THE METRO

Finished size: 20˝ × 20˝

Stitch up this simple, clean-lined modern pillow for the man in your life. Made in solid fabrics with bold white sashing, it'll look great in his "man cave"—or in your living room!

Materials and Supplies

COORDINATING SOLIDS: a variety
totaling ½ yard*

LINEN SCRAP: at least 2½˝ × 2½˝

SOLID NEUTRAL: ½ yard for sashing and borders

MUSLIN: 22˝ × 22˝ for pillow top lining

BATTING: 22˝ × 22˝

BACKING: ½ yard of 42˝-wide fabric

DISAPPEARING-INK OR CHALK MARKER
to mark quilting lines

PILLOW FORM: 20˝ × 20˝

* I used Robert Kaufman's Kona Cotton Solids, so the color names of these fabrics are used in the instructions.

ARTIST: *Jen Carlton Bailly*
WEBSITE: bettycrockerass.com

Jen is a self-taught sewist. Before she began sewing she graduated from the Art Institute of Seattle in Fashion Marketing. Having a love of textiles, fashion and art, sewing/quilting was a natural progression and a quick addiction. Becoming involved in the Modern Quilt Guild and the first president of the Portland Chapter opened up a whole new culture to her. She finds inspiration in everything from an old dresser drawer to a run down Portland building. Currently a stay-at-home mom, she spends her time sewing during nap time and whenever she can squeeze it in.

Cutting

BLACK, HONEY, AMBER,
MOCHA, EARTH, COFFEE:

Cut coordinating solid
pieces using sizes given
in the layout diagram at
right. Label the pieces as
you cut. (I use blue painter's
tape to stay organized.)

LINEN SCRAP:

Cut 1 piece 2½˝ × 2½˝.

SOLID NEUTRAL:

Cut 2 pieces 1½˝ × 20½˝.

Cut 5 pieces 1½˝ × 18½˝.

Cut 1 piece 2½˝ × 5½˝.

Cut 1 piece 1½˝ × 10½˝.

Cut 4 pieces 1½˝ × 2½˝.

Cut 2 pieces 1½˝ × 3½˝.

Cut 1 piece 1½˝ × 11½˝.

INSTRUCTIONS

All seam allowances are ¼˝.

1. Arrange pieces as shown.

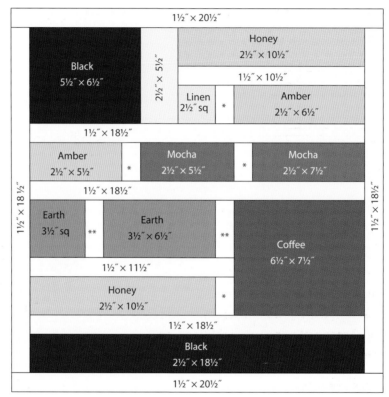

* 1½˝ × 2½˝

** 1½˝ × 3½˝

2. Sew pieces together in sections as shown below; sew the sections together. Press the seams as you prefer; I press mine to the side.

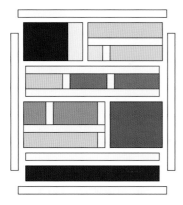

3. Sew the 1½˝ × 18½˝ borders to the sides, and then sew the 1½˝ × 20½˝ borders to the top and bottom. Press.

4. Layer muslin lining, batting, and pieced pillow top; baste. Using a ruler and chalk or a disappearing-ink marker, draw quilting lines. I randomly drew straight lines, as shown below.

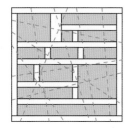

5. Using a walking foot if you have it—otherwise a regular foot is fine—quilt the pillow top, following the lines you've drawn. Increase the stitch length to 8 stitches per inch, or at least 2 settings past the stitch length you use for piecing.

6. Trim the layers to square up the pillow top to 20½˝ × 20½˝.

7. Choose a backing option from Pillow Construction Techniques (page 116). Make the pillow backing and sew it to the pillow top using a ¼˝ seam allowance.

Featuring large-scale print

PHOTOGENIC

Finished size: 20˝ × 20˝

This easy-to-make pillow is the perfect way to showcase either an embroidery design or a beautiful large-scale print. As shown, the embroidered version features a lovely flower, but the pillow also would look great with an embroidered silhouette of someone you love. Then the corner triangles would be like photo corners!

Materials and Supplies

To feature a large-scale print:

LARGE-SCALE PRINT: 1 fat quarter for center block

To feature embroidery:

SOLID FABRIC: 1 fat quarter for center block

EMBROIDERY FLOSS: 1 skein (6-ply) in a complementary color

EMBROIDERY NEEDLE

EMBROIDERY TRACING PAPER

FOR BOTH VERSIONS:

ADDITIONAL PRINTS: scraps totaling ¼ yard for the remaining pieces

BACKING: ½ yard of 42˝ fabric

BINDING: 1 piece 2½˝ × 21˝ for double-fold binding, or purchased binding*

BATTING: 22˝ × 22˝

TAILOR'S CHALK OR FABRIC MARKER

PILLOW FORM

* I love the look of a print binding, so I prefer to make my own.

ARTIST: *Mo Bedell*
WEBSITE: limegardenias.blogspot.com

Mo grew up always in the pursuit of something creative. Earning a degree in fine arts helped to formalize her creativity, and she could not be more thrilled that she now earns a living doing the things that have brought her joy throughout her life. Mo currently designs fabrics with Andover and sews as much as she can. She lives in the beautiful Pacific Northwest with her husband and two children.

Cutting

Center block featuring large-scale print:

PRINT 1 (LARGE-SCALE PRINT): Cut 1 piece 13″ × 15″.

Center block featuring embroidery:

SOLID FABRIC: Cut 1 piece 13″ × 15″.

For both versions:

BACKING: Cut 2 pieces 14″ × 20½″.

REMAINING PRINTS: Cut 2 pieces 4″ × 5″ for corner border blocks.

Cut 2 pieces 4″ × 17¼″ for top and bottom borders.

Cut 2 pieces 5″ × 15″ for side borders.

Cut 2 pieces 6½″ × 6½″ for corner triangles.

Featuring embroidery

INSTRUCTIONS

Construction is the same whether you feature a large-scale print or embroidery.

All seam allowances are ⅜″ except as noted for the final pillow assembly.

Making the Pillow Top

1. On the 13″ × 15″ piece, measure 5¼″ from each corner on all sides; make a dot with a pencil or chalk. Using a ruler and a rotary cutter, cut from dot to dot.

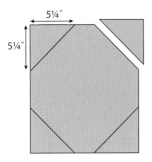

2. Cut both of the 6½″ × 6½″ squares in half diagonally to make 4 triangles.

3. With right sides together, place a triangle as shown, points extending. Sew and press. Repeat for each corner. The center section should measure 13″ × 15″.

4. Sew a 5″ × 15″ strip to each side of the center section; press.

5. Sew a 4″ × 5″ piece to the left side of a 4″ × 17¼″ piece. Sew this border to the top, lining up the block at the left end with the vertical strip below. Sew the other 4″ × 5″ piece to the right side of the remaining 4″ × 17¼″ piece. Sew to the bottom of the center section. Press.

For the embroidered version, copy the embroidery pattern (page 21) at 200%. Center a sheet of embroidery tracing paper over the center block, transfer side down, and position the pattern on it. Pressing firmly, trace to transfer the pattern to the fabric. Carefully put the block in an embroidery hoop or frame and embroider it using a split stitch— each stitch comes up between the strands of the stitch before it, creating a neat line.

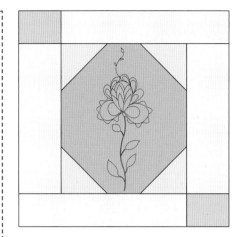

Quilting and Finishing

1. Layer the batting and the pieced pillow top. I tape my batting to the table and make sure it's smooth; then I place the finished block on top and secure with safety pins every 5˝.

2. Quilt the pillow top. I used straight-line stitching in the borders and triangles, and outlined the center section. Square up the pillow top to 21˝ × 21˝, trimming so the block remains nicely centered.

3. For the pillow backing, follow the instructions for Envelope Backing with Binding in Pillow Construction Techniques (page 117).

Photogenic

Enlarge 200%.

Featuring large-scale print

CHEVRONS

Finished size: 18½˝ × 18½˝

Here's a fresh interpretation of the classic chevron motif. A shot of bright yellow in an otherwise neutral palette is like a cheery exclamation point, an automatic mood elevator. Half-square triangles form the basis of this pillow's construction.

Materials and Supplies

YELLOW PRINTS: scraps from 2 different fabrics

LIGHT SOLIDS: scraps from 2 or 3 different fabrics

LINEN SCRAP: at least 3½˝ × 3½˝

NEUTRAL PRINTS: scraps from 7 or 8 fabrics

DARK PRINTS: scraps from 2 or 3 fabrics

SOLID BLACK: ⅛ yard for inner border

LIGHT PRINT: ⅛ yard for outer border

BATTING: 20˝ × 20˝

BACKING: ½ yard

PILLOW FORM: 18˝ × 18˝

ARTIST: *Brooke Biette*
WEBSITE: apriltwoeighty.com

Brooke enjoys the brightest and boldest fabrics she can get her hands on, often using a modern style with a pinch of vintage. She recently helped to open a sewing lounge, The Atelier Stitch, in Portland, Maine. She has taught beginning, advanced, and some paper piecing quilting classes. When she's not tossing fabric around the room, hoping it will fall in the perfect grouping, she's dying her hair purple, or daydreaming of her faux boyfriend Adam Levine. Sometimes she does all three with her three cats as witnesses.

Cutting

YELLOW PRINTS:
Cut 5 squares 3½˝ × 3½˝.

LIGHT SOLIDS:
Cut 18 squares 3½˝ × 3½˝.

LIGHT PRINTS:
Cut 12 squares 3½˝ × 3½˝.

DARK PRINTS:
Cut 2 squares 3½˝ × 3½˝.

BLACK SOLID:
Cut 2 strips 1˝ × 15½˝.

Cut 2 strips 1˝ × 16½˝.

LIGHT PRINT:
Cut 2 strips 2˝ × 16½˝.

Cut 2 strips 2˝ × 19½˝.

INSTRUCTIONS

All seam allowances are ¼˝.

Making the Pillow Top

1. Pair each light solid with a yellow print, light print, or dark print. Make half-square triangle blocks, as described in Half-Square Triangles (page 120). It is possible to chain piece these blocks, and it's quicker!

2. Square up each half-square triangle block to 3˝ × 3˝ to ensure accuracy.

3. Arrange the blocks to form the chevron pattern, following the assembly diagram.

> **Note:** *You will have a dark print block and another block left over, which you can incorporate into the pillow backing or use to make a pincushion!*

4. Sew the blocks for each row. Press the seams of each row in alternate directions.

5. Sew the rows together, nesting seams pressed in opposite directions and carefully matching intersections with triangle points. The chevron block should measure 15½˝ square.

6. For the inner border, sew the shorter black strips to the sides first, and then sew the 2 longer black strips at the top and bottom.

7. Repeat Step 6 for the light print outer border, adding sides first, then top and bottom. The pillow top should measure 19½˝ square.

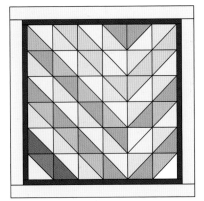

Assembly diagram

Quilting and Finishing

1. Layer the pillow top facing right side up on the batting; baste.

2. Using a neutral-colored thread, quilt ¼˝ on both sides of each chevron seam. Quilt along the inner edge of the outer border, and again ¼˝ from that line.

3. To finish the pillow, follow the instructions in Pillow Construction Techniques (page 116) using the backing and closure of your choice. Use a ½˝ seam to attach the backing to the pillow top.

LIFE AQUATIC

Finished size: 18˝ × 18˝

Complementary colors—opposites on the color wheel—give this pillow its zing. A tangerine cross floats on a sea of aqua, surrounded by sand-colored linen. It may be the next best thing to a day at the beach!

ARTIST: *Heather Bostic*
WEBSITE: alamodefabric.blogspot.com

For Heather's profile, see page 5.

Materials and Supplies

AQUA: scraps in assorted values totaling ¼ yard

TANGERINE: scraps in assorted tones for cross

LINEN: ¼ yard for border

BACKING: ½ yard home decorating fabric

BATTING: 20˝ × 20˝

MUSLIN: 20˝ × 20˝ for pillow top lining

PILLOW FORM: 18˝ × 18˝

Cutting

AQUA: Cut 44 squares 2½˝ × 2½˝.

TANGERINE: Cut 5 squares 2½˝ × 2½˝.

LINEN: Cut 2 strips 3˝ × 14˝.

Cut 2 strips 3˝ × 19˝.

BACKING: Cut 2 rectangles 14˝ × 19˝.

INSTRUCTIONS

Seam allowances are ¼", unless otherwise noted.

1. Arrange the 2½" × 2½" squares on a flat surface, placing the tangerine squares in a cross, as illustrated.

2. Sew 7 squares to form a strip. Repeat to make a total of 7 strips, pressing seams in opposite directions for each strip.

3. Sew the 7 strips together into a block, nesting seams that were pressed in opposite directions. Pin to ensure precise intersections.

4. Square up the block to 14" × 14", trimming the outer squares so that the patchwork block remains centered.

5. Sew the 3" × 14" linen strips to the top and bottom of the patchwork block; press the seams. Sew the remaining linen strips to the sides; press. The pillow top should measure 19" × 19".

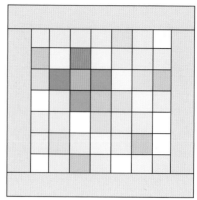

Assembly diagram

6. Sandwich the muslin lining, batting, and pillow top. Baste using your preferred method.

7. Quilt in an aesthetic design of your choice. I used a light-colored thread to create an additional layer of design—another "plus" that extends the patchwork "plus"—and then machine quilted with ¼" rows of straight stitching.

8. Prepare and attach the pillow back, referring to the instructions in Pillow Construction Techniques (page 116). Use a ½" seam to sew the backing to the pillow top.

Life Aquatic

GUMDROP

Finished size: 20¼″ × 20¼″

Fanciful circles seem to be layered on top of one another, creating the illusion of depth in this stylized Candy Land. Intricate fabric patterns play off one another to add texture and movement along with a sense of playfulness.

Materials and Supplies

ASSORTED NEUTRALS: 9 squares 8″ × 8″, or ½ yard

ASSORTED COLOR PRINTS: 9 squares 6½″ × 6½″, or ⅜ yard

BACKING AND BINDING: 1 yard linen

BATTING: 22″ × 22″

MUSLIN: 22″ × 22″, for pillow top lining

PILLOW FORM: 20″ × 20″

WATER-SOLUBLE FABRIC MARKER

ARTIST: *Heather Bostic*
WEBSITE: alamodefabric.blogspot.com

For Heather's profile, see page 5.

Cutting

USE THE GUMDROP
TEMPLATE PATTERNS (PAGE 122).

ASSORTED NEUTRALS:

Trace 9 concave pieces, using the water-soluble pen and template. Cut out the pieces.

ASSORTED COLOR PRINTS:

Trace 9 convex pieces, using the water-soluble pen and template. Cut out the pieces.

BINDING:

Cut 3 strips 2½˝ × 40˝ for double-fold binding.

BACKING:

Cut 2 rectangles 15˝ × 20¾˝.

INSTRUCTIONS

This pillow top has 9 blocks sewn from curved pieces.

All seam allowances are ¼˝ unless otherwise noted.

Assembling the Pillow Top

1. Press the 9 convex pieces in half, wrong sides together. Press the 9 concave pieces in half, right sides together. The creases will provide a guide for matching the curved seams.

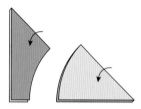

2. With right sides together, place a concave piece on a convex piece, matching the creases. Place a pin at the crease and continue around the curve, placing pins a finger's width apart.

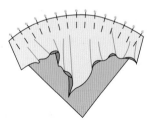

3. Sew a ¼˝ seam, backstitching at the beginning and end. Press toward the concave piece. Repeat for the remaining 8 blocks.

4. Trim the 9 blocks to 7¼˝ × 7¼˝, keeping the convex portion of the block intact.

5. Sew the 9 blocks together into the pillow top.

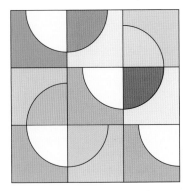

tip *Pin to ensure that seams line up precisely, paying special attention to matching the curved sections so that the resulting circles will look continuous.*

Quilting and Finishing

1. Layer the muslin lining, batting, and pieced pillow top. Baste, using your preferred method.

2. Quilt in the design of your choice. I used ½˝ straight-stitch machine quilting to contrast with and emphasize the circle design element.

3. Sew the pillow backing as described in Pillow Construction Techniques, Envelope Backing with Binding (page 117) and Double-Fold Straight-Grain Binding (page 119).

UNION JACK

Finished size: 20″ × 20″

Here's to another fabulous example of a British invasion. Muted tones with a smart design give this cushion an intelligent feel for your favorite hipster. It just feels good going international.

Materials and Supplies

LINING FABRIC: 1 yard

9 ASSORTED LIGHT PRINTS: scraps at least 3″ × 7¼″ for background of Union Jacks

3 GRAY PRINTS: 1 fat eighth each

CREAM SOLIDS: ¼ yard

LINEN: ¼ yard

BACKING: ¾ yard of 42″-wide fabric

BATTING: 20″ × 20″

BINDING: 3 strips 2½″ × width of fabric (WOF)

PILLOW FORM: 20″ × 20″

ARTIST: *Tacha Bruecher*
WEBSITE: fatquarterly.com

Tacha is a quilt designer and teacher who is well known in the online quilting community as a founding member of the *Fat Quarterly* e-zine. She has published many patterns and articles as part of *Fat Quarterly*, as well as patterns in *Sew Hip* magazine. Tacha is the author of *Hexa-Go-Go*, a book of modern English paper-pieced hexagon quilts, from Stash Books, an imprint of C&T Publishing. She lives in Berlin, Germany, with her husband and two daughters.

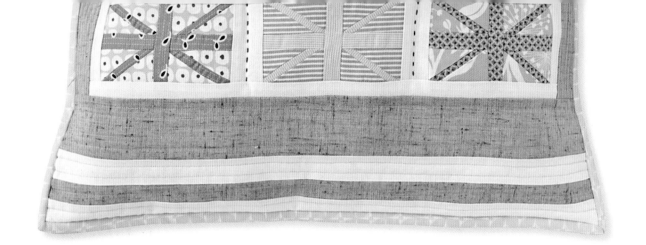

Cutting

ASSORTED LIGHT PRINTS:

From each of the 9 prints, cut 4 rectangles 2¾˝ × 1¾˝, for 36 pieces total.

GRAY PRINTS:

From each of the 3 prints, cut 12 strips ¾˝ × 4˝, 6 strips 1˝ × 2½˝, and 3 strips 1˝ × 3˝.

CREAM SOLID:

Cut 6 strips 1½˝ × 3˝.

Cut 2 strips 1½˝ × 16˝.

Cut 2 strips 1˝ × 10˝.

Cut 2 strips 1˝ × 17˝.

Cut 4 strips 1½˝ × 20½˝.

LINEN:

Cut 2 strips 2¼˝ × 11˝.

Cut 2 strips 2½˝ × 20½˝.

Cut 2 strips 1¼˝ × 20½˝.

LINING FABRIC:

Cut 1 square 24˝ × 24˝.

Cut 1 piece 15˝ × 20½˝.

Cut 1 piece 18˝ × 20½˝.

BACKING FABRIC:

Cut 1 piece 15˝ × 20½˝.

Cut 1 piece 18˝ × 20½˝.

INSTRUCTIONS

Seam allowances are ¼˝, unless otherwise noted.

Making the Union Jack Blocks

1. Take 2 rectangles that were cut from the same light print for the Union Jack background, and cut them in half diagonally from the top left to the bottom right. Cut the other matching light print rectangles from the top right to the bottom left.

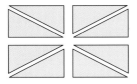

2. Sew a gray ¾˝ × 4˝ strip between each set of triangles to make 4 pieced rectangles.

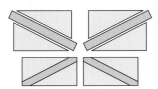

3. Press the seams and trim the rectangles to 1½˝ × 2½˝.

4. Using 2 gray 1˝ × 2½˝ strips and a gray 1˝ × 3˝ strip, sew the rectangles together as shown. Repeat with all 9 prints to make 9 Union Jack blocks. Each Union Jack block should measure 3˝ × 5˝.

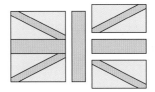

Assembling the Pillow Top

1. Arrange the Union Jack blocks in a 3 × 3 layout.

2. Sew the 1½˝ × 3˝ cream strips and Union Jack blocks into rows. Press the seams.

3. Sew the 1½˝ × 16˝ cream strips between the rows. Press the seams.

4. Sew a 1˝ × 10˝ cream strip to each side. Press. Sew a 1˝ × 17˝ cream strip to the top and the bottom. Press.

5. Sew a 2¼˝ × 11˝ linen strip to each side. Press the seams. Sew a 2½˝ × 20½˝ linen strip to the top and the bottom.

6. Sew a 1½˝ × 20½˝ cream strip to the top and the bottom.

7. Sew a 1¼˝ × 20½˝ linen strip to the top and the bottom.

8. Sew a 1½˝ × 20½˝ cream strip to the top and the bottom of the block. The pillow top should measure 20½˝ × 20½˝.

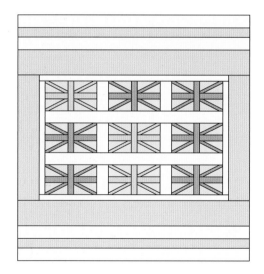

Quilting and Finishing

1. Layer the 22˝ × 22˝ lining, the batting, and the completed pillow top. Baste. Quilt as desired. Trim all layers to a 20½˝ × 20½˝ square.

2. To prepare the pillow backing, follow Steps 1–3 of Envelope Backing with Lining (page 117).

3. Pin the lined backing pieces to the pillow top, right sides facing out, so that they are aligned at the outer edges and overlap in the middle. Sew the pillow top to the backing, ⅛˝ from the edge.

4. Prepare the binding and bind the pillow, following the instructions for Double-Fold Straight-Grain Binding (page 119). Insert the pillow form.

Union Jack

CRIMSON STONES

Finished size: 19½˝ × 19½˝

I love reinterpreting traditional blocks with new variations and modern fabrics. This project, based on the traditional Bright Hopes block, introduces a technique that may be new to some—partial seams. You'll be amazed at how quickly and easily these blocks go together using this method.

ARTIST: *Joan Callaway*
WEBSITE:
wishestrueandkind.blogspot.com

Materials and Supplies

PRINTS: ⅛ yard, or scraps to make 20 rectangles 2˝ × 4½˝ and 4 squares 3˝ × 3˝

GRAY* SOLID: ¼ yard

WHITE SOLID: ⅛ yard

BACKING: ½ yard of 42˝ fabric

MUSLIN: 22˝ × 22˝ for lining

BATTING: 22˝ × 22˝

PILLOW FORM: 20˝ × 20˝

* I chose Kona Coal as my neutral for this pillow because I love the way it makes the saturated colors of Anna Maria Horner's Innocent Crush print fabrics pop.

Cutting

PRINT FABRICS: Cut 20 rectangles 2˝ × 4½˝.

Cut 4 squares 3˝ × 3˝.

GRAY FABRIC: Cut 16 rectangles 2˝ × 4½˝.

Cut 5 squares 3˝ × 3˝.

Cut 2 strips 1¾˝ × 18˝.

Cut 2 strips 1¾˝ × 20½˝.

WHITE FABRIC: Cut 2 strips 1˝ × 17˝.

Cut 2 strips 1˝ × 18˝.

BACKING FABRIC: Cut 2 rectangles 14˝ × 20½˝.

Joan has been interested in needle arts since early childhood. Inspired by her mother's love of sewing, Joan started with various types of embroidery and needlepoint, which eventually led to her love of fabric and quilting. Despite working full time as a pediatric speech-language pathologist and infant-toddler mental health specialist, she is a passionate evening and weekend quilter. Joan enjoys sewing with friends in her sewing circle, interacting with other quilters online, and maintaining her blog. Her work has been featured on other blogs and websites, and "Wishes, True and Kind" was chosen as one of *Quilter's Home* magazine's 55 favorite blogs of 2010. Joan is a member of the Portland Modern Quilt Guild and served as its first secretary. She lives in Hillsboro, Oregon.

INSTRUCTIONS

Seam allowances are ¼˝ unless otherwise specified.

Making the Bright Hopes Blocks

1. Arrange the 3˝ × 3˝ squares and 2˝ × 4½˝ rectangles to form 9 blocks, as shown; 4 blocks have print centers and 5 blocks have gray centers.

2. Sew the blocks using the partial seams method outlined below.

PARTIAL SEAMS METHOD

1. With right sides together, sew rectangle 1 partially to the right side of the center square (about 1½˝). Press this partial seam toward the rectangle. (Figure A)

2. Sew rectangle 2 to the top of the block. Press toward the rectangle. (Figure B)

3. Sew rectangle 3 to the left of the block. Press toward the rectangle. (Figure C)

4. Sew rectangle 4 to the bottom of the block. Pressing toward the rectangle. (Figure D)

5. Fold rectangle 2 to reveal the partial seam. Align the edge of rectangle 1 with the block edge. Start sewing a few stitches before the end of the partial seam to secure, and then sew the remaining seam. (Figure E)

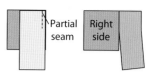

Partial seam · Right side

Figure A

Figure B

Figure C

Figure D

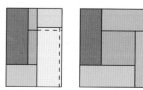

Figure E

Assembling the Blocks

1. Arrange the blocks on a design wall or other flat surface, alternating blocks with gray centers to make 3 rows of 3 blocks.

2. Sew the rows together. Press the seams in rows 1 and 3 in the same direction. Press the seams in row 2 in the opposite direction.

3. Sew the rows together, nesting seams pressed in opposite directions. Press.

4. Sew the 1″ × 17″ white border strips to the sides of the pillow top. Press the seams toward the borders.

5. Sew the 1″ × 18″ white border strips to the top and bottom of the pillow top. Press toward the borders.

6. Sew the 1¾″ × 18″ gray border strips to the sides of the pillow top. Press toward the borders.

7. Sew the 1¾″ × 20½″ gray border strips to the top and bottom of the pillow top. Press toward the borders. The pillow top should measure 20½″ × 20½″, allowing for ½″ seams when attaching the backing.

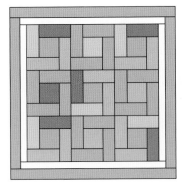

Assembly diagram

Quilting and Finishing

1. Layer and baste the muslin, batting, and pillow top. Quilt as desired, by hand or machine.

2. Make an envelope backing for the pillow, referring to the instructions in Pillow Construction Techniques (page 116).

LOVE NOTE

Finished size: 17½˝ × 17½˝

Nothing is sweeter than a love note. The sunny sentiment on this pillow could be your handmade heartfelt message to a special friend—or use this same technique to write your own love notes using favorite quotes or words.

ARTIST: *Amber Carrillo*

WEBSITE:

oneshabbychick.typepad.com

Amber lives on the North Shore of Oahu with her husband and four children. A stay-at-home mom who loves sewing and soccer (they go together, right?), Amber discovered the online world of sewing blogs and fabric stores about four years ago and has been sewing madly every since. She loves fabric, and most afternoons you can find her in her little sewing space, listening to audio books as she sews.

Materials and Supplies

BACKGROUND: fat quarter of fabric that looks like notebook or graph paper, or a solid*

ASSORTED COLORS: scraps totaling ¼ yard, for appliqués

YELLOW: 5˝ × 5˝ scrap for sun appliqué

DOUBLE-SIDED FUSIBLE WEBBING: 12˝ × 20˝ (I like HeatnBond or Steam-A-Seam2)

MUSLIN: 20˝ × 20˝ for pillow top lining

AIR-SOLUBLE MARKING PEN

BATTING: 20˝ × 20˝

BACKING: ½ yard

PILLOW FORM: 18˝ × 18˝.

* There are lots of fun Japanese import fabrics that look like lined paper; look for them online.

Cutting

USE THE LETTER TEMPLATE PATTERNS (PAGE 123).

BACKGROUND:

Cut a piece 18˝ × 18˝.

FUSIBLE WEBBING:

Cut 16 pieces 3˝ × 4˝.

Cut a circle 4½˝ in diameter.

INSTRUCTIONS

All seam allowances are ¼˝.

Making the Letter Appliqués

1. Iron a 3˝ × 4˝ piece of fusible webbing to the wrong side of each of the fabric scraps, following the manufacturer's instructions. Don't peel off the paper backing yet.

2. Trace the letter templates onto the paper side of the fused fabric. The letters will be backward. Cut out each letter.

3. Arrange the letters to spell "You are my sunshine," as shown in the photo, making sure to leave room for the sun. When you are satisfied with the placement, remove the paper backing and iron the letters in place.

4. Iron the fusible webbing circle to the wrong side of the yellow fabric circle; don't peel off the paper backing yet. Position the circle on the background fabric, leaving room to quilt "rays" around the sun. Remove the paper backing and iron in place.

Quilting and Finishing

1. Layer the muslin lining, batting, and appliquéd pillow top (right side up). Baste or use a few safety pins to keep the layers from shifting.

2. With a marking pen, draw a spiral on the yellow circle, starting in the middle and winding out to the edges.

3. Using white thread and a free-motion or darning foot, lower the feed dogs and sew along the marked lines, starting in the center. Tie off the starting and ending threads by pulling the top threads through to the lining. Trim any loose threads.

> **tip** *To remove the paper from the back of the appliqué pieces, use a seam ripper to make a tiny tear in the paper so you can easily pull it off without distorting or fraying the fabric appliqué.*

4. Using black thread and a free-motion or darning foot with the feed dogs lowered, sew around the yellow circle. Repeat 2 or 3 times for a strong outline. Tie off the threads.

5. Draw lines out from the circle, alternating between short and long rays. Using black thread, sew along these lines once or, for more definition, 2 or 3 times. Tie off the threads.

6. Using black thread, free-motion stitch around each letter 2 or 3 times. The stitches should catch just inside the fabric edge. Your stitching is supposed to be a bit imperfect, so relax and have fun! Tie off the threads.

7. Finish the pillow with an envelope backing, as described in Pillow Construction Techniques (page 116). Use a ¼˝ seam to attach the backing to the pillow top.

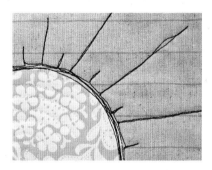

SATELLITE

Finished size: 17½˝ × 17½˝

With its mod vibe and its rich texture and color palette, the Satellite pillow could easily be the star attraction in any room in your home. Fussy cutting the appliqué pieces to take advantage of the fabric motif multiplies the impact of this design.

Materials and Supplies

SOLID: 1 yard for pillow top background and backing

PRINT: ⅛ yard for small appliqués

FUSIBLE WEBBING: ¼ yard

TEMPLATE PLASTIC

MUSLIN: 20˝ × 20˝

BATTING: 20˝ × 20˝

BINDING: ⅛ yard

PILLOW FORM: 18˝ × 18˝

ARTIST: *Brioni Greenberg*
WEBSITE: flossyblossy.blogspot.com

Brioni lives in Leeds, United Kingdom, with a gorgeous American bloke, a cute and feisty little boy named Jack, two kitties, and 33 Strawberry Shortcake dolls. She has been sewing on and off for most of her life; her first sewing machine was a Holly Hobbie windup model. She got her first "grown-up" sewing machine when studying textile design and technology in college. Brioni had always wanted to make a patchwork quilt and finally bit the bullet about five years ago, never imagining that it would lead to the biggest obsession she's ever had!

Cutting

USE TEMPLATE PATTERNS A, B, C, AND D (PAGE 125).

SOLID BACKGROUND: Cut 1 square 19″ × 19″ for pillow top.

Cut 2 rectangles 12″ × 18″ for backing pieces.

TEMPLATE PLASTIC: Cut 1 each of template patterns A, B, C, and D.

PRINT: Adhere fusible web to print fabric, following the manufacturer's instructions. Cut appliqué pieces from the fused fabric, and if desired, choose specific motifs printed on the fabric as I've done:

Cut 8 of template A.

Cut 9 of template B.

Cut 8 of template C.

Cut 8 of template D.

LINING FOR BACKING: Cut 2 rectangles 12″ × 20″.

BINDING: Cut 2 strips 2¼″ × WOF for double-fold binding.

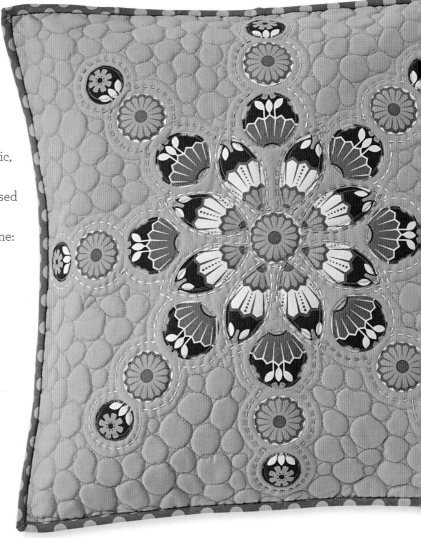

INSTRUCTIONS

Making the Pillow Front

1. Fold the 19˝ × 19˝ square of background fabric in half widthwise; press. Fold in half again, this time lengthwise; press. Unfold the fabric.

2. Remove the paper backing from the fusible web and position the appliqué pieces on the background fabric, as shown in the photo. Use the pressed lines as guides to space pieces evenly. The outer pieces should be at least 1˝ from the edge.

3. Once you are happy with the placement, press to adhere the pieces to the background fabric.

4. Trim the pillow top to 18˝ × 18˝.

Quilting and Finishing

1. Prepare the pillow top for quilting by marking a line ¼˝ from the outer edge of the entire motif; draw a second line ¼˝ outside the first line. Draw a line ⅛˝ around each petal.

2. Layer and baste the batting and pillow front. Quilt the outer marked line by machine. Quilt the inner line and the lines around the petals by hand, using embroidery floss and a running stitch.

3. Fill in the area outside the motif by machine, using a design of your choice. I quilted pebbles for my pillow.

4. Using the 12˝ × 18˝ rectangles of background and lining fabric, prepare the pillow backing according to the directions for Envelope Backing with Lining (page 117).

5. Pin the lined backing pieces to the pillow top, right sides out, aligning outer edges. The backing pieces will overlap in the middle. Using a walking foot, sew around the pillow with a ⅛˝ seam to secure all the layers.

6. Prepare the binding and bind the pillow, following the directions in Double-Fold Straight-Grain Binding (page 119).

7. Insert the pillow form.

JEWEL OF THE SEA

Finished size: 16½″ × 16½″

Meant to dazzle, this cushion accomplishes its intricate design through the use of a paper-pieced foundation—making it possible to sew narrow strips of fabric into blocks. Chances are, you'll quickly become addicted to this method of quilting.

ARTIST: *Shelly Greninger*
WEBSITE:
pinkpunkshelly.blogspot.com

Shelly is a working mom of three school-age children. She started sewing when she was a teenager but drifted from it until she wanted to make money at home. She started making and selling purses on Etsy in 2009 before opening her own shop, Pink Punk Boutique. She closed her shop recently to work outside the home again but still does some custom work. Inspired by Flickr groups and swaps, she quilts and does smaller sewing projects as often as she has a chance. She is an avid reader, so when not working, taking care of her family, or sewing, chances are she's curled up under her Bliss quilt with her Kindle in hnad.

Materials and Supplies

PRINTS: a variety of scraps at least 10″ long

WHITE SOLID: ⅓ yard for borders

AQUA SOLID: 1 yard for block center strips, borders, backing, and binding

MUSLIN: 1 yard for pillow top lining and backing lining

BATTING: 19″ × 19″

PRINTER PAPER: 4 pieces 6″ × 6″

GLUESTICK

PILLOW FORM: 16″ × 16″

Cutting

ASSORTED PRINTS:
Cut 15 strips 1½″ × 10″.

Cut strips in widths varying from ¾″ to 1¼″, in lengths varying from 2″ to 9″ for string blocks.

WHITE SOLID: Cut 4 strips 1½″ × 13″.

Cut 4 strips 1¼″ × 17½″.

AQUA SOLID: Cut 4 strips 1″ × 9″.

Cut 4 strips 1¼″ × 14″.

Cut 2 strips 2½″ × WOF.

Cut 2 pieces 15″ × 19″.

INSTRUCTIONS

All seam allowances are ¼˝.

Making the String Blocks

1. Use a gluestick to adhere a 1˝ × 9˝ aqua solid strip, right side facing up, to each of the 4 paper squares. Center the strips on the diagonal.

2. Set the machine's stitch length to 1.5 (be sure to set it back again when you are finished with these blocks). Select one of your various-width print fabric strips, and place it right side down on the center fabric, raw edges together. Sew in place. Press right side out.

3. Work your way to the corner, sewing strips and pressing, varying the prints and colors however you like. Then turn the block around and fill the other side the same way.

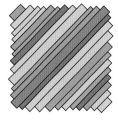

4. When all 4 blocks are covered with strips, flip them over so you can see the paper. Use a ruler to square up each block to 6˝ × 6˝, and then tear the paper away from the seams.

5. Cut each block into quarters so that you have 16 small string blocks, each 3˝ × 3˝.

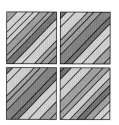

Assembling the Blocks

1. Arrange the string blocks into a 4 × 4 pattern. You can rotate the 8 blocks with aqua solid centers to form either a diamond or an X pattern. Sew the blocks together in 4 rows. Press the seams, pressing alternate rows in opposite directions.

2. Sew the rows together, being careful to match up the seams. Press the seams open.

3. Sew a 13˝ white solid strip to each side, trimming off the excess at the ends. Press the seams away from the center. Sew a white solid strip to the top and bottom.

4. Repeat Step 3 using the aqua solid strips. Trim the pillow top to 13½˝ × 13½˝.

5. To create the patchwork border, sew the 15 print strips together along the 10˝ sides. Press all the seams in the same direction.

6. Use a ruler and rotary cutter to straighten the ends, and then cut the unit into 4 strips 1½˝ wide. This will give you 4 strips of 15 mini-blocks. Remove 2 blocks from the end of 2 of the strips so that you have 2 strips with 15 blocks and 2 strips with 13 blocks.

7. Sew a 13-block patchwork strip to each side. Sew a 15-block strip to the top and bottom, being careful to match up the seams on the corner blocks.

8. Sew the last set of white solid strips to the sides first, then to the top and bottom. Trim the pillow top to 17˝ × 17˝.

Assembly diagram

Quilting and Finishing

1. Layer the muslin, batting, and pillow top; baste in your preferred manner. Quilt the pillow top by hand or machine.

2. Make your preferred pillow backing out of the darker solid fabric, referring to the instructions in Pillow Construction Techniques (page 116).

3. To create a quilted backing for your pillow, repeat Step 1 with the backing you have prepared.

4. Pin the lined backing pieces to the pillow top, right sides out, aligning outer edges. Sew around the pillow with a ⅛˝ seam to secure all the layers.

5. Bind the pillow with the darker solid fabric. Insert the pillow form.

*Pillow*POP

VIOLET CATHEDRAL

Finished size: 18¾″ × 18¾″

Cathedral Window, a quilt design inspired by stained-glass windows, offers endless options for choosing colors to carry out the theme. This sophisticated violet version is distinguished by a particularly striking color scheme.

ARTIST: *Terri Harlan*
WEBSITE: sew-fantastic.blogspot.com

Materials and Supplies

GRAY LINEN: 3 yards for cathedral windows and backing

VIOLET: a variety of solids and prints totaling ⅜ yard

CARDBOARD OR TEMPLATE PLASTIC: 13½″ × 13½″ square

FABRIC MARKER: I used a Pilot FriXion pen (heat removes marks)

BUTTONS: 13 violet ½″ size

PILLOW FORM: 18″ × 18″

Cutting

GRAY LINEN: Cut 9 squares 15″ × 15″.

VIOLET FABRICS: Cut 24 squares 4″ × 4″.

Terri has been exploring sewing of all kinds since she was fifteen. A wife and the mother to a spicy four-year-old girl, she recently moved with her family to sunny California. Sewing is a calming hobby and even became an at-home business about five years ago when Terri left her corporate job. The online community has been inspirational to her—she finds the friendly support amazing and is so glad to be a part of it.

INSTRUCTIONS

All seam allowances are ¼˝.

1. Mark a 15˝ gray square ¾˝ from each edge on the wrong side of the fabric. Place the template inside this line. Press the corners in first; then fold the sides. To find the center, fold the square in half from top to bottom, then from side to side, and press, keeping the ¾˝ turned under.

2. Bring each corner to the center of the square. Press, taking time to keep the new corners as neat as possible.

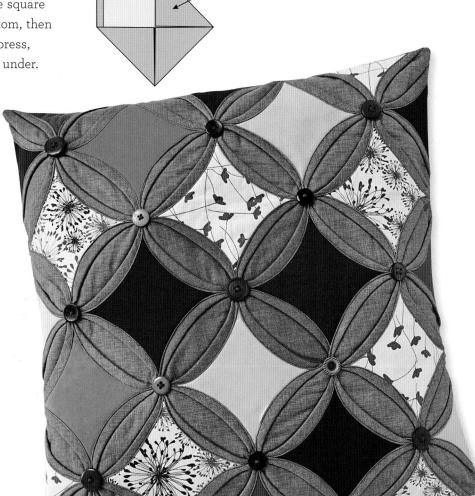

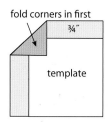

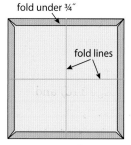

3. Fold each corner to the center again. This will give you a folded block measuring about 6¾″ × 6¾″. Make 9 of these blocks.

4. Place 2 blocks side by side and lift the adjacent folded triangles, aligning edges at the top and bottom, and pin. Sew along the fold line through both triangles.

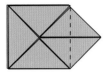

5. Make and attach each of the 9 blocks in the same way, to create the 3 × 3 layout.

6. The diamond shapes that are between the blocks are the "windows." Center the violet 4″ × 4″ squares on these windows. The violet square will not cover the entire gray area. Fold the gray edges over the violet square in an arch shape to cover the square, and pin. Sew along the edge of the arch, for all 4 sides.

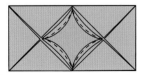

7. Repeat Step 6 to create each window. The windows at the outer edge will hang over the sides of the pillow top.

8. Attach buttons in each of the 13 places where the arched windows come together.

9. Along the sides of the pillow, trim the violet fabric that hangs over, being careful not to cut into the gray linen folds.

10. To finish the pillow, refer to Pillow Construction Techniques (page 116) and make an envelope backing using the remaining gray linen for the backing pieces. Use a ¼″ seam when sewing the backing pieces to the pillow top.

*Pillow*POP

A BUNCH OF CROSSES

Finished size: 20″ × 20″

This pillow is super-simple to construct—it's composed entirely of 2½″ × 2½″ squares. You just have to pay attention to the layout of the squares in order to achieve the desired cross patterns. Small- and medium-scale prints or solids work best for the design; this pattern is also a perfect way to make use of scraps left over from other projects. Why not try varying shades of a single color for a subtle look in a modern home, or bright primary colors for a fun pillow in a child's bedroom? The possibilities go on and on!

ARTIST: *Katy Jones*
WEBSITE: fatquarterly.com
ImAGingerMonkey.blogspot.com

Katy is one of the four founding members of the modern quilting e-zine *Fat Quarterly*. Katy and the rest of the FQ team met on Flickr, and although they all live in different parts of the world, they have come together with a common love of the online quilting community and each other's aesthetics. Katy's personal mantra is that there is no such thing as ugly fabric, and she will try her hardest to include at least one "ugly" in everything she makes.

Materials and Supplies

ASSORTED PRINTS AND SOLIDS: 6 fat eighths

BACKING: ½ yard of 42″ fabric

BINDING: ¼ yard

MUSLIN: 22″ × 22″ for pillow top lining

BATTING: 22″ × 22″

BUTTON FOR PILLOW BACK (optional)

PILLOW FORM: 20″ × 20″

Cutting

ASSORTED PRINTS AND SOLIDS:
Cut 20 squares 2½″ × 2½″ from each fabric (there will be leftovers).

BACKING:
Cut 2 pieces 14″ × 20½″.

BINDING:
Cut 3 strips 2½″ × 40″ for double-fold binding.

INSTRUCTIONS

All seam allowances are ¼˝ unless otherwise stated.

Assembling the Squares

1. On a design wall or table, lay out the 2½˝ × 2½˝ squares in 10 rows of 10 squares, referring to the assembly diagram. Move the squares around to form the crosses in a pleasing arrangement. Take care not to place fabrics that are too similar next to each other. Remove the leftover squares.

2. Sew the squares together in rows, checking after each row that no squares have accidentally skipped to the wrong place. It's helpful to stack the squares in order by row and to mark the top of each row with a Post-it.

3. Press the seams open, and then sew row 2 to row 1, row 3 to row 2, and so on.

4. Press the seams open and give the completed pillow top a good pressing all over.

Assembly diagram

Quilting and Finishing

1. Mark quilting designs on the pillow top, or plan to stitch without marking.

2. Layer and baste the lining fabric, batting, and pillow top. Quilt the layered pillow sandwich. I used dense quilting with straight lines on my pillow. I marked only the center and then used the edge of the walking foot as a guide for the remaining lines.

3. Trim all layers to 20½″ × 20½″.

4. Make a buttoned back closure as outlined in Pillow Construction Techniques (page 117).

5. Pin the lined backing pieces to the pillow top, right sides facing out, so they are aligned at the outer edges and the backing pieces overlap. Sew the pillow top to the backing, ⅛″ from the edge.

6. Bind, following the instructions in Double-Fold Straight-Grain Binding (page 119). Insert the pillow form.

COSMOS

Finished size: 20˝ × 20˝

*Layered hexagons form the petals of the bright posy
blooming on this pillow top. The hexagon borders use
1930s fabrics, but in a fresh, modern setting.*

Materials and Supplies

BLUE: ⅝ yard for pillow front and back

PRINTS: scraps totaling ¾ yard

FUSIBLE BATTING: ¼ yard

PERLE COTTON THREAD for decorative stitching

PIPING: ¼ yard

COTTON CORDING: 2¼ yards of ¼˝-diameter cording

INVISIBLE ZIPPER: 20˝ length

PILLOW FORM: 20˝ × 20˝

ARTIST: *Jessica Kovach*
WEBSITE: twinfibers.blogspot.com

Sewing and quilting have been great
ways for **Jessica** to have a creative
outlet as a stay-at-home mom of three.
With her sister, she started a blog a few
years ago to stay motivated to finish projects. Along the way, she's participated in
many quilting bees, swaps, and books,
and those always inspire her to try a new
technique or something she's thought up.
Being creative with sewing has provided
her with much happiness, and her hope
is to inspire others to find joy in sewing
as well.

Cutting

Use hexagon template patterns A and B (page 124).

BLUE: Cut 2 squares 21˝ × 21˝.

PRINTS: Cut 7 squares 5˝ × 5˝; from these, cut 7 template A hexagons (sides are 2¼˝).

Cut 7 squares 9˝ × 9˝; from these, cut 7 template B hexagons (sides are 4˝).

PIPING: Cut 2 strips 2˝ × WOF.

FUSIBLE BATTING: Cut 7 template A hexagons.

tip *You can use nonfusible batting, but pin the layers securely together.*

INSTRUCTIONS

Assembling the Flower

1. Cut the center hexagon out of template B to use this template as a positioning guide.

2. Place a large fabric hexagon (cut from template B) wrong side facing up; position template B on it as a positioning guide.

3. Place a hexagon of fusible batting in the template opening, and then lay a small fabric hexagon on top, right side up. Remove the template. Press the 3 layers with an iron to fuse the batting.

4. Fold a side of the outer hexagon, using the small hexagon as the fold line, and press. Unfold. Fold, press, and unfold each side.

5. Fold the raw edge of the border fabric to the fold created in Step 4. Press. Proceed all the way around the hexagon.

6. Fold the border fabric once again, creating a finished edge, and pin. Edgestitch as shown.

7. Repeat Steps 1–6 for the remaining 6 hexagons.

8. Hand stitch the hexagons together to create a flower.

9. Position the flower on the blue background piece, 2½˝ from the bottom edge and 2½˝ from the left edge. Pin. Edgestitch in place. Add a decorative running stitch around the flower with perle cotton thread.

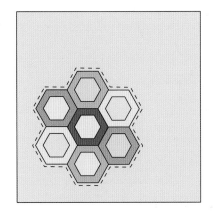

Adding the Piping

1. Join the 2 lengths of piping fabric using a diagonal seam, as in Step 1 of Double-Fold Straight-Grain Binding (page 119).

2. Fold the piping fabric around the cording and sew close to the cording using a zipper foot.

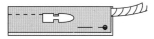

3. Place the piping on the pillow top, aligning raw edges, and pin. Sew with a ½˝ seam allowance, leaving the first inch of the piping loose so that you can attach it to the end later. Clip the piping seam allowance at the corners so the seam lies flat.

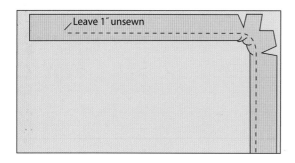

4. To join the ends of the piping: First, remove a few stitches at the end to reveal the cording. Then cut the cording so the ends meet; wrap piping fabric as shown, pin, and sew.

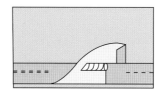

Finishing

Insert a zipper and attach the backing, referring to the directions under Zipper Backing (page 118) in Pillow Construction Techniques.

69

Cosmos

SNOWFLAKE

Finished size: 20˝ × 20˝

Modern chic with a simple elegance, this Snowflake pillow can be transformed into any season by changing the petal colors. Winter, spring, summer, or fall—each can find a home in this design.

ARTIST: *Jessica Kovach*
WEBSITE: twinfibers.blogspot.com

For Jessica's profile, see page 65.

Materials and Supplies

DARK GRAY SOLID OR NEAR-SOLID*: ⅝ yard, for pillow background and backing

BLUE SOLIDS*: scraps from 5 shades totaling ⅓ yard, and 1 fat quarter of another blue, for petals and pillow back

SEW-IN LIGHTWEIGHT INTERFACING: 18˝ × 20˝ piece

BATTING: 22˝ × 22˝

MUSLIN: 22˝ × 22˝ for pillow top lining

PILLOW FORM: 20˝ × 20˝

I used Robert Kaufman's Quilter's Tweed in Pepper and Kona Cotton Solids in shades of blue.

Cutting

DARK GRAY:
Cut 1 square 21˝ × 21˝.

BLUE SOLIDS:
Cut 24 rectangles 2˝ × 5˝.

INTERFACING:
Cut 24 rectangles 2˝ × 5˝.

INSTRUCTIONS

Assembling the Pillow Front

Use the Snowflake petal template pattern (page 125).

1. Trace the snowflake petal template on the wrong side of each blue solid rectangle.

2. Place a blue solid rectangle, wrong side up, on an interfacing rectangle. Using a very small stitch length, sew on the traced line. Trim the seam allowance to a scant ⅛˝, tapering the seam allowances at the petal points, as shown. Make 24 petals.

3. Cut a slit in the interfacing and turn the petal right side out, using a point turner or blunt needle to reach into the point. Press.

4. Lightly press the dark gray background square in half horizontally and vertically to find the center. Using the fold lines as a guide, arrange the petals as shown. Place the 6 petals in the center to position the petals that form the circle.

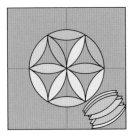

5. Remove the 6 petals in the center and arrange them outside the circle, along with the rest of the petals, and pin. Appliqué the petals in place using a decorative blanket stitch.

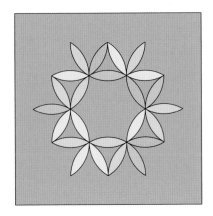

Quilting and Finishing

1. Layer the muslin lining, batting, and pillow top; baste. Sew the layers together, ¼˝ from the edge.

2. Use the remaining dark gray solid and the blue fat quarter to make the backing—see Envelope Backing (page 116). Sew the backing to the pillow front.

X's & O's

Finished size: 24″ × 16½″
(16½″ × 16½″ without flanges)

This pillow is all about the details—intricately patterned fabrics, graceful flange closures, fabric-covered buttons. The clever design makes a great showcase for special prints.

ARTIST: *Kelly Lautenbach*
WEBSITE:
kellylautenbach.typepad.com

Kelly loves life as a wife and empty nester. She spends her days pretending to run her husband's business and regularly sneaks over to her sewing studio. As dinnertime nears, she slips back out to the "real world" to do just enough to make it look as if she's worked all day. Shhhhhhh! Please don't tell. When she's not sewing, she enjoys living the good life in Nebraska and playing Gram to the world's cutest little boy, Sutton.

Materials and Supplies

SOLID AQUA: 1½ yards for background, flanges, and pillow back

CIRCLE FABRIC: 1 fat eighth print

"X" FABRIC: ⅛ yard

BORDER: 1 fat quarter

MUSLIN: 20″ × 20″ for pillow top lining

BATTING: 20″ × 20″

PILLOW FORM: 16″ × 16″

6 BUTTONS: 1¼″ size (I made fabric-covered buttons using a kit)

Cutting

SOLID AQUA:
Cut 1 square 12″ × 12″.

Cut 2 squares 17½″ × 17½″.

Cut 2 rectangles 8½″ × 33½″.

CIRCLE FABRIC:
Cut 1 circle with a diameter of 7½″.

"X" FABRIC:
Cut 2 strips 2″ × 19″ (the remaining fabric will be used to cover the buttons).

BORDER:
Cut 2 strips 3″ × 12½″.

Cut 2 strips 3″ × 17½″.

INSTRUCTIONS

All seam allowances are ¼˝ unless otherwise noted.

Assembling the Pillow Front

1. Center the 7½˝ circle on top of the 12˝ × 12˝ solid aqua square. To find the center, fold both the circle and the square into quarters and lightly press. Match the fold lines, and pin. Sew around the circle with a zigzag stitch to attach.

2. Lay the circle-in-square piece on a cutting mat and cut diagonally from the bottom left corner to the top right corner.

3. Sew an "X" strip between the 2 halves. Leave plenty of strip fabric at both ends so you can square up the block after both "X" strips are sewn. Press the seam allowances toward the "X" strip.

4. Take the block back to the cutting mat and cut diagonally again, this time from the bottom right corner to the top left corner.

5. Sew the second "X" strip, again leaving extra fabric at both ends. Press toward the "X" strip.

6. Square up the block to 12½″ × 12½″. Sew the 12½″ borders to the sides of the block. Press. Sew the 17½″ border strips to the top and bottom. Press. Square up the block to 17½″ × 17½″.

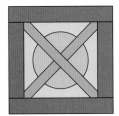

Assembly diagram

Quilting and Finishing

1. Layer the muslin, batting, and pillow top; baste. Quilt as desired. I quilted in the ditch along all seams and around the circle.

2. Layer the 2 square 17½″ × 17½″ solid aqua backing pieces wrong sides together, and stitch them together to form a substantial backing for your pillow, using a quilting pattern of your choice—I quilted diagonal lines to form squares that sit on point.

3. With right sides together, sew the pillow top to the pillow back at the *top and bottom only*, using a ½″ seam allowance.

4. For the flanges, create 2 tubes by sewing the 8½″ × 33½″ strips, right sides together, along the 8½″ sides. Turn and fold, creating a large tube 4¼″ wide. Press well, placing the seam in the middle of the back, forming creases where the flange will meet the top and bottom of the pillow.

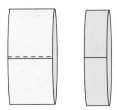

5. Make 3 horizontal buttonholes on the front of each flange, about 2″ away from the raw edges. Space them 4″ from the top, 4″ from the bottom, and in the center.

6. Follow the covered button kit instructions to make 6 buttons, and sew the buttons to the inside back of the flange.

7. Pin the flanges around the sides of the pillow top, using the creases to match the top and bottom. Sew with a ½″ seam allowance. Press the seam toward the pillow.

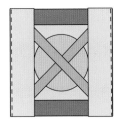

8. Insert the pillow form and button the sides closed.

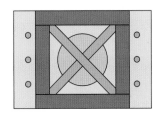

CANDY-COATED DIAMONDS

Finished size: 16˝ × 16˝

Retro has never looked so chic as in this eye-catching design with its saturated colors. Paper piecing is the secret to making the diamond blocks with their angled borders.

ARTIST: *Penny Layman*
WEBSITES:
sewtakeahike.typepad.com
sew-ichigo.blogspot.com

Materials and Supplies

PRINTS: scraps totaling ¼ yard for diamond centers

SOLIDS: ¼ yard each of 3 different colors for diamond borders (I used blue, green, and tan.)

BATTING: 19˝ × 19˝

BACKING: ⅜ yard

BINDING: ¼ yard

PILLOW FORM: 16˝ × 16˝

Cutting

PRINTS:
Cut 40 squares 2½˝ × 2½˝.

SOLIDS:
Cut into strips 1½˝ × WOF.

BACKING:
Cut 2 pieces 12˝ × 18˝ for the envelope back.

BINDING:
Cut 2 strips 3½˝ × WOF.

Penny lives in Colorado and loves to keep active with whitewater kayaking, hiking, backpacking, and car camping with her husband Lenny. She is a lover of foundation piecing and designs quirky, fun patterns. She teaches paper piecing to large and small groups and loves to impart her skill to her students. You can find her at sewtakeahike.typepad.com and her paper piecing blog, sew-ichigo.blogspot.com, where she is a co-owner/designer.

INSTRUCTIONS

All seam allowances are ¼˝, unless otherwise specified.

Paper Piecing the Diamonds

Use the Candy-Coated Diamonds template pattern (page 125).

1. Trace 40 diamonds onto foundation paper (or thin paper) using the template, and cut out the diamonds.

2. Paper-piece the 40 diamonds: Start with the print in the center square and follow the piecing order in the template, cutting border pieces as you go. There are 16 blue, 12 tan, and 12 green diamonds. Leave a ¼˝ seam allowance on all sides of the template.

Sewing the Diamonds Together

1. Arrange the diamonds using the assembly diagram to guide the color placement—the diamond border colors should form rows going across.

2. Sew the diamonds into diagonal strips. There are 2 strips each with 2, 4, 6, and 8 diamonds. Use the paper templates to match seams. Press seams in opposite directions for each row.

3. Sew the strips together to create the pillow top, nesting seams that were pressed in opposite directions.

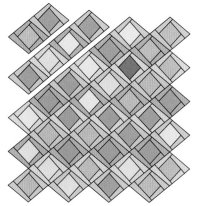

Assembly diagram

4. Starch and press. Remove the paper and trim to 17˝ × 17˝.

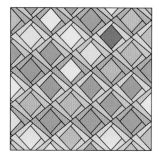

Quilting and Finishing

1. Place the pieced pillow top on the batting. Quilt by stitching in the ditch around the diamonds. Trim the batting.

2. Using the 2 backing pieces, follow the instructions in Envelope Backing (page 116).

3. Pin the backing pieces to the pillow top, right sides facing out, aligning the outer edges and overlapping the backing pieces. Baste around the pillow ¼˝ from the edge.

4. Sew the 3˝-wide binding strips together in a diagonal seam as described in Step 1 of Double-Fold Straight-Grain Binding (page 119). Sew the binding to the *back* of the pillow top using a ½˝ seam allowance. Fold the binding to the front, press, and edgestitch. Insert the pillow form.

Candy-Coated Diamonds

CRYSTALLIZED

Finished size: 20˝ × 20˝

With its kaleidoscopic burst of color, this pillow brings a smile to the face and instant cheeriness to whatever room it brightens. Contrasting warm and cool tones give the pillow its vibrancy and sense of movement.

Materials and Supplies

WARM-COLORED PRINTS: scraps totaling ½ yard of red, pink, yellow, and orange

COOL-COLORED PRINTS: scraps totaling ½ yard of green, blue, and purple

BATTING: 22˝ × 22˝

PRINT BACKING: ½ yard, with 42˝ usable width

PILLOW FORM: 20˝ × 20˝

Cutting

WARM-COLORED PRINTS: Cut 50 squares 3˝ × 3˝.

COOL-COLORED PRINTS: Cut 50 squares 3˝ × 3˝.

BACKING: Cut 2 rectangles 15˝ × 21˝.

ARTIST: *Angela Mitchell*
WEBSITE: fussycut.blogspot.com

Angela lives in northwest Pennsylvania. She shares her home with her husband and children, and together they run a small hobby farm. Once an elementary school teacher, she currently spends her days at home with her three kids. Angela is a self-taught crafter who has been sewing for more than twelve years. Her favorite things to design and create are quilts and pillows.

INSTRUCTIONS

All seam allowances are ¼˝.

Making the Pillow Top

1. Pairing warm with cool squares, make 100 half-square triangles as described in Half-Square Triangles (page 120). Square them up to 2½˝ × 2½˝.

2. Arrange the half-square triangles in 10 rows, positioning blocks to form rings of warm and cool colors.

Assembly diagram

3. Sew the blocks for each row together. Press all seams for row 1 in the same direction, all seams for row 2 in the opposite direction, and so on. This will help when joining rows in the next step.

4. Sew the 10 rows together, nesting the seams pressed in opposite directions. Press.

Quilting and Finishing

1. Layer the completed pillow top over the batting; baste.

2. Quilt straight lines along the warm-colored triangles ¼˝ from the seams.

3. Trim both layers to 20½˝ × 20½˝.

4. Create an envelope backing as described in Pillow Construction Techniques, Envelope Backing (page 116). Sew the backing to the pillow top using a ¼˝ seam.

Crystallized

SUNBURST

Finished size: 18¼˝ × 18¼˝

This jaunty take on the Dresden Plate pattern presents its stylized symmetry as a bright-hued fabric bouquet. Depending on the color palette, the same design can fit a conservative, traditional decorating scheme as easily as a dramatic, contemporary one.

ARTIST: *Angela Mitchell*
WEBSITE: fussycut.blogspot.com

For Angela's profile, see page 83.

Materials and Supplies

BLUE TONAL: 1 fat eighth for Sunburst Circle

WHITE SOLID: 1 fat eighth for Sunburst Circle backing

ASSORTED PRINTS: scraps totaling ½ yard for wedges

GRAY SOLID: 1 yard for background and backing

BATTING: 20˝ × 20˝

BINDING: ¼ yard

PILLOW FORM: 18˝ × 18˝

Cutting

ASSORTED PRINTS:
Cut 10 rectangles 7˝ × 9˝.

GRAY SOLID:
Cut 1 square 18¾˝ × 18¾˝ for pillow front.

Cut 2 rectangles 11˝ × 20˝ for pillow back.

BINDING:
Cut 2 strips 2½˝ × 40˝ for double-fold binding.

INSTRUCTIONS

Use the Sunburst Circle and Sunburst Wedge templates patterns (page 126).

All seam allowances are ¼˝.

Sewing the Sunburst Circle

1. Enlarge and trace the Sunburst Circle template onto the wrong side of the blue circle fabric. Place the blue fabric on the white square, right sides together, and sew on the line. Trim, leaving a ¼˝ seam allowance. Notch or pink the edges.

2. Cut an opening near the middle of the white circle, being careful not to cut into the blue fabric. Turn the blue circle right side out.

White fabric trimmed back

3. Trim the white fabric back, leaving about ½˝. Push out the circle, and press.

Sewing the Wedges

1. Trace the wedge template 2 times on the wrong side of each of the 10 print 7˝ × 9˝ rectangles. Cut out 20 wedges.

2. Fold a wedge in half, right side facing in, and sew across the top. Finger-press the seam open.

3. Turn the wedge right side out. Push out the corner, center the seam, and press. Make a total of 20 wedges.

4. Sew the wedges together into 4 sets of 5, sewing from the wider end of the wedge to the unfinished end. Sew 2 sets together to create a half circle; repeat for the other half. Sew the 2 halves together. Press the seams in the same direction.

5. To find the center of the gray background, fold the 18¾˝ × 18¾˝ square in quarters, lightly press, and unfold. Using the creases as a guide, place the Sunburst wedges on the gray background. Pin in place.

6. Sew around the outside with a blanket stitch to attach the wedges to the background. If you prefer, use a straight, zigzag, or satin stitch.

7. Center the circle on top of the wedges. Sew it in place the same way you attached the wedges.

Quilting and Finishing

1. Layer and baste the batting and the Sunburst pillow top.

2. With gray thread, using the edge of a walking foot attachment as your guide, sew around the inside and outside of the circle. Then quilt inside and outside the wedges in the same manner. Continue echo-quilting outward to the edges of the pillow top.

3. Trim the excess batting.

4. Prepare the envelope backing sections as described in Pillow Construction Techniques, Envelope Backing (page 116). Pin the backing pieces to the pillow top, right sides facing out, overlapping the backing pieces. Baste ¼˝ from the edge.

5. Attach double-fold binding as described in Double-Fold Straight-Grain Binding (page 119). Insert the pillow form through the envelope opening.

*Pillow*POP

GRAPHIC JUXTAPOSITION

Finished size: 17½″ × 17½″

This graphic pillow packs a big punch by combining a fun fabric with textural felted wool from an old woolen sweater. (Look for one in a thrift store!) This lets you mix colors, textures, and prints in one simple design. The heft of the felted sweater material works well with the quilted panel of a home decorating-weight or cotton canvas print. If you can't find a sweater to match a fabric you want to use, substitute woolen yardage—or pull out the needles and some 100% wool worsted yarn and create your own piece.

Materials and Supplies

GRAPHIC-PRINT HOME DECORATING-WEIGHT FABRIC: ⅜ yard*

FELTED WOOL FROM RECYCLED SWEATER: 6″ × 18½″ after felting; instructions follow

MUSLIN: ½ yard for lining

BACKING: ⅜ yard home decorating-weight fabric

BATTING: 20″ × 30″

PILLOW FORM: 18″ × 18″

The graphic-print directional fabric in my pillow looks like multiple fabrics sewn together, but it's actually just one!

ARTIST: *Kirsten Ott*
WEBSITES:

threedancingmagpies.blogspot.com
threedancingmagpies.etsy.com

Kirsten embraces a variety of forms of creative expression, including knitting, jewelry making, metalworking, photography, quilting, and sewing. These endeavors have led her to operate a small yarn shop, write knitting patterns, teach both sewing and knitting classes, and run a small jewelry and craft supply business. Her work has been sold in small boutiques, online, and at art and craft shows. She learned to quilt three years ago and loves the inspiration of online swaps and the wonderful sense of community provided by the modern quilting blog world.

Cutting

GRAPHIC PRINT:
Cut 1 piece 14˝ × 19˝
for main panel.

MUSLIN:
Cut 1 piece 15˝ × 20˝.

BACKING:
Cut 2 pieces 12˝ × 18½˝.

BATTING:
Cut 2 pieces 15˝ × 20˝.

THE FELTING PROCESS

(Recycle a Wool Sweater)

To felt the wool, start with a 100% wool sweater—or portion of a sweater—that is at least 50% larger than the final size needed for the project. Put the sweater in the washing machine with a pair of jeans and run the wash cycle using hot water, but remove the wool before the spin cycle. The jeans provide needed friction during the felting process. Washing machines and wools both vary in their behavior, so this may require experimentation.

Rinse the sweater, spread it on a towel, and blot the excess water. Once it's dry, felted wool can be cut with a rotary cutter or scissors, so use it as you would any other fabric.

INSTRUCTIONS

All seam allowances are ½˝.

1. Make a quilt sandwich with the main panel: Place the lining fabric on the bottom, 2 batting layers in the middle, and the 14˝ × 19˝ graphic print on top.

2. Using a walking foot, quilt as desired. I quilted straight lines and varied the space between lines to add visual interest.

3. Trim the quilted piece to 13½˝ × 18½˝.

4. With right sides together, pin the quilted piece to the felted wool along the long side. Sew, and press the seam toward the quilted side.

5. Quilt 2 lines of topstitching, the first ¼˝ from the seam and the second ¼˝ from the first line, to secure the felted wool.

6. Finish the pillow using an Envelope Backing technique (page 116).

FLYING RAINBOW

Finished size: 17˝ × 17˝

I'm sure you have a lot of scraps lying around, as I do, so why not showcase some of them in this fun Flying Geese pillow? Arrange them in a rainbow-color order, like the pillow shown here, or use shades of a single color for a monochromatic interpretation of the design. You'll soon be seeing lots of possibilities in your scrap bin!

Materials and Supplies

PRINTS: scraps totaling ¼ yard in all 7 rainbow colors: red, orange, yellow, green, blue, indigo, and violet

WHITE SOLID: ½ yard for background

MUSLIN: ⅝ yard for pillow top lining

BACKING: ½ yard

BINDING: ¼ yard

BATTING: 20˝ × 20˝

PILLOW FORM: 16˝ × 16˝

ARTIST: *Amanda Sasikirana*
WEBSITE:
amandasasikirana.wordpress.com

Amanda lives in Ohio with her husband, two kids, and beloved sewing machine. She's always looking for clever ways to use up her never-ending supply of fabric scraps. Other than that, she teaches sewing classes at a local fabric shop, knits scarves and hats, and plays with Blythe dolls.

Cutting

PRINTS: From each of the 7 colors, cut 7 rectangles 1½˝ × 3½˝, for 49 pieces in all.

WHITE SOLID: Cut 14 squares 3˝ × 3˝.

Cut 1 rectangle 8½˝ × 17½˝.

Cut 1 rectangle 5½˝ × 17½˝.

MUSLIN: Cut 1 square 20˝ × 20˝.

BACKING: Cut 2 rectangles 14˝ × 19˝.

BINDING: Cut 2 strips 2½˝ × 40˝ for double-fold binding.

INSTRUCTIONS

All seam allowances are ¼˝.

Making the Pillow Top

1. Sew 6 of the 7 red pieces to make a strip, reserving a red piece for the binding. Repeat with all the other colors to make 7 pieced rectangles. Trim the rectangles to 3˝ × 5½˝.

2. Using the pieced rectangles and the 14 white 3″ × 3″ squares, make 7 Flying Geese units according to the directions in Flying Geese (page 121). Each Flying Geese unit should measure 3″ × 5½″.

3. Sew the Flying Geese units into a row in rainbow-color order: red, orange, yellow, green, blue, indigo, violet.

4. Sew the white 8½″ × 17½″ rectangle to the top of the Flying Geese row. Sew the 5½″ × 17½″ rectangle to the bottom. Press the seams open.

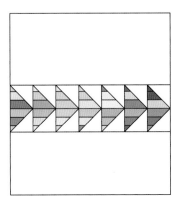

Quilting and Finishing

1. Layer the muslin, batting, and pieced pillow top. Baste, and quilt as desired. Trim the pillow top to 17½″ × 17½″.

2. Construct an envelope backing, following the directions in Pillow Construction Techniques (page 116).

3. Pin the backing pieces to the pillow top, right sides facing out, overlapping the backing pieces. Baste ¼″ from the edge.

4. To make the pieced binding, sew together the 7 reserved color pieces along their long sides in rainbow-color order; press the seams open. Trim to 2½″ × 7½″. Sew a binding strip to each end of the pieced rectangle; press the seams open.

5. Attach the binding as directed in Double-Fold Straight-Grain Binding (page 119), referring to the photograph for placement of the rainbow strip. Insert the pillow form.

DON'T BE SQUARE

Finished size: 19½˝ × 19½˝

Squares of color encircle this crisp white pillow top, but don't be fooled by the simplicity of the color scheme—the seemingly plain background is an intricate patchwork of white pieces.

Materials and Supplies

WHITE SOLID: ¾ yard

PRINTS: scraps in various colors—I used red, pink, orange, yellow, green, blue, brown, and gray

BATTING: 22˝ × 22˝

BINDING: ¼ yard

BACKING: ½ yard

PILLOW FORM: 20˝ × 20˝

ARTIST: *Erin Singleton*
WEBSITE: twomoreseconds.com

Erin started sewing and quilting furiously after her son was born six years ago and has barely slowed down since. A blogger for more than twelve years, she jumped in with both feet when she found the online sewing community and became involved in virtual quilting bees, swaps, and sewing blogs. To create a place for her online friends to meet in person, she founded the Sewing Summit conference in 2010.

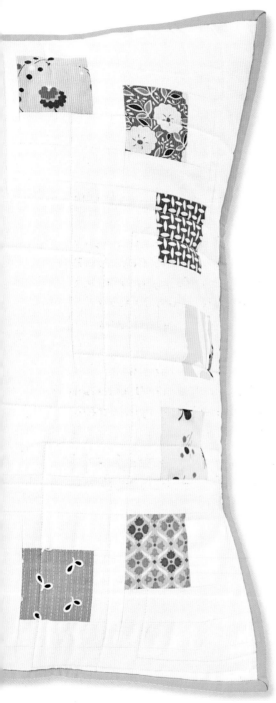

Cutting

WHITE: Cut 3 strips 2½˝ × WOF; subcut as follows, labeling pieces as you go:

LABEL	CUT	SIZE
A	2	2½˝ × 20½˝
B	12	2½˝ × 1½˝
C	4	2½˝ × 2½˝
D	4	2½˝ × 4½˝

Cut 4 strips 1½˝ × WOF; subcut as follows, labeling pieces as you go:

LABEL	CUT	SIZE
E	4	1½˝ × 5½˝
F	4	1½˝ × 4½˝
G	24	1½˝ × 3½˝
H	2	1½˝ × 10½˝

Cut 1 rectangle 8½˝ × 12½˝. Label this piece I.

PRINTS: Cut 16 squares 2½˝ × 2½˝ (2 each from 8 colors).

BINDING: Cut 3 strips 2½˝ × 40˝ for double-fold binding.

INSTRUCTIONS

All seam allowances are ¼˝, and all seams are pressed open unless otherwise noted.

Assembling the Pillow Top

Assemble the pillow top in 3 sections, laying out each section and following the piecing order in the illustrations.

SECTION 1

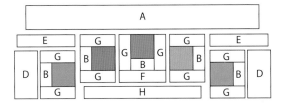

1. Sew B rectangles (see cutting instructions for rectangle sizes) to each of the 5 red, pink, and orange squares in Section 1. Press the seams toward the color squares.

2. Sew G rectangles to both sides of each unit from Step 1.

3. Sew an F rectangle to the bottom of a pink unit from Step 2. Add a red unit (from Step 1) to the left, a pink unit to the right, and then an H rectangle to the bottom. Use the assembly diagram to make sure you rotate the color units as needed.

4. Sew a D rectangle to the left of the remaining red unit, and another D to the right of the orange unit. Sew E rectangles to the top of these 2 units.

5. Sew together the units from Steps 3 and 4, and then sew an A rectangle to the top to complete Section 1.

SECTION 2

1. Sew a C square to a gray, a brown, an orange, and a yellow square. Press the seams toward the color squares.

2. Sew a B rectangle to a gray square; sew a B rectangle to a yellow square. Following the assembly diagram for Section 2, sew G rectangles to each side of the gray unit and to each side of the yellow unit. Sew F rectangles to the left of the gray unit and to the right of the yellow unit.

3. Sew together the units from Steps 2 and 3, using the assembly diagram for color placement and rotation.

4. Sew the units from Step 4 to the left and right of the 8½˝ × 12½˝ piece to complete Section 2.

SECTION 3

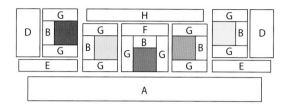

Section 3 is constructed in the same way as Section 1, but turned upside down to complete the color circle. Follow the assembly diagram for Section 3 and use the piecing technique from Section 1, keeping in mind the correct rotation and color placement.

JOINING THE SECTIONS

Sew Sections 1, 2, and 3 together. Square up the pillow top to 20˝ × 20˝.

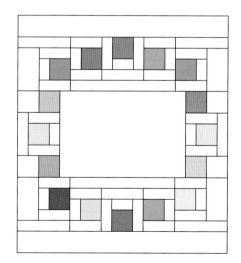

Quilting and Finishing

1. Layer and baste the batting and pillow top. Quilt by hand or machine—I quilted straight lines that form rectangles and squares, to repeat the square design.

2. Construct an envelope backing as described in Pillow Construction Techniques, Envelope Backing (page 116).

3. Pin the backing pieces to the pillow top, right sides facing out, overlapping the backing pieces. Baste ¼″ from the edge.

4. Make and attach the binding as described in Double-Fold Straight-Grain Binding (page 119). Insert the pillow form.

*Pillow*POP

FRESH BLOOM

Finished size: 21″ × 21″

Bursting with color, this pillow top utilizes an easy raw-edge appliqué process that assures you of a one-of-a-kind piece. Plan out your color scheme, or use this as a scrap-busting project.

Materials and Supplies

APPLIQUÉ FABRICS: scraps totaling ½ yard

FOUNDATION FABRIC: ⅝ yard linen or linen blend

BORDER: ¼ yard

LIGHTWEIGHT DOUBLE-SIDED FUSIBLE WEBBING: ¾ yard

MUSLIN: 23″ × 23″

BATTING: 23″ × 23″

PRESSING CLOTH: to protect your iron from sticky adhesive

BACKING: ½ yard for envelope closure, or see Pillow Construction Techniques (page 116) for closure of your choice

PILLOW FORM: 20″ × 20″

ARTIST: *Ryan Walsh*
WEBSITES: patchworksquared.com
ryanwalshquilts.com

Ryan is a self-taught quilter and quilt designer who enjoys giving a modern twist to classic quilt designs. He is a licensed funeral director in the Catskill Mountain region of New York. A busy dad of three, the majority of his quilting adventures occur in the late hours of the night after his kids are in bed. Quilting helps satisfy his never ending need to be creative. Ryan's work combines traditional piecing methods with free-style construction techniques. As a way to challenge his ability, he participates in online bees and quilt-related swaps. He's contributed patterns to several quilting books and magazines.

Cutting

FOUNDATION FABRIC: Cut 1 square 20˝ × 20˝.

BORDER: Cut 2 strips 1½˝ × 20˝.

Cut 2 strips 2½˝ × 22˝.

INSTRUCTIONS

Use the circle template patterns (page 127).

All seam allowances are ¼˝.

Creating the Appliqué Design

Most double-sided fusible webbing has 3 layers: an adhesive layer between 2 layers of nonstick paper.

1. You will create the appliqué design starting from the center. Choose 5 fabrics for the flower center, and follow the manufacturer's instructions to fuse the fabric, wrong side down, to the fusible webbing. Use a pressing cloth to protect your iron.

2. Using the 1˝ circle template, mark the paper side of the 5 fused fabrics you chose for the center flower, and cut on the marked line.

3. Find the center of the foundation fabric by folding it in half, pressing, and unfolding. Lay a ruler along the crease line and mark 10˝ from the edge with a pencil or fabric pen.

4. Remove the paper backing from a 1˝ appliqué circle to expose the webbing; place the appliqué over the center mark. Fuse, following manufacturer's instructions and using a pressing cloth to protect your iron.

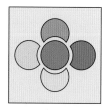

5. Nest and fuse 4 more 1˝ circles around the first circle. To create a nesting edge, overlap the circles, trace the outline of the bottom circle onto the top circle, and trim the top circle along the line.

6. Continue to build your design outward by randomly nesting and fusing circle appliqués. I used more than 80 circles in my design. You can use the 3˝ and 4˝ templates provided or create circles ranging in size from 2˝–4˝ to build your design. Stop adding appliqué circles ¼˝ from the edge of the foundation.

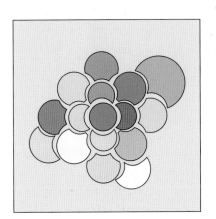

Attaching the Borders

1. Sew the 1½˝ × 20˝ border strips to the top and the bottom. Press the seams toward the border.

2. Sew the 1½˝ × 22˝ borders to the sides. Press the seams toward the border.

Quilting and Finishing

1. Secure the appliqué circles to the foundation by stitching ⅛˝ from their outside edges.

2. Layer and baste the muslin, batting, and pillow top.

3. Select and create a closure for the pillow back, using Pillow Construction Techniques (page 116).

URBAN SEAWEED

Finished size: 20″ × 20″

This pillow project is perfect for those times when you need to come up with a quick gift; you can easily stitch it together in an afternoon. It can be made in a variety of color combinations, but try to pick a contrasting background so that your prints pop out against the solids or near-solids. Can't make up your mind which fabrics to use? Make two. Or three!

Materials and Supplies*

PRINTS: scraps totaling ⅓ yard

BLUE SOLID: ⅓ yard

GRAY SOLID: ¾ yard for border and backing

MUSLIN: 23″ × 23″ for pillow top lining

BATTING: 23″ × 23″

PILLOW FORM: 20″ × 20″

* I used Patty Young's fabric line called "Sanctuary" in teal and gray hues. For the background and envelope backing, I used Robert Kaufman's Quilter's Linen.

ARTIST: *Karrie Winters*
WEBSITE: FreckledWhimsy.com

Karrie has been sewing for more than thirteen years and loves it even more today than ever. After dabbling in sewing clothing, she now makes mostly quilts and pillows of all sizes. In the last year, she has designed her own patterns and tutorials for Moda Bake Shop, Robert Kaufman, and Riley Blake Designs.

Cutting

PRINTS:

Cut 19 rectangles 2½˝ × 4½˝.

BLUE SOLID:

Cut 6 strips 1½˝ × WOF; subcut into 6 pieces 1½˝ × 14½˝, 6 pieces 1½˝ × 2½˝, 8 pieces 1½˝ × 4½˝, and 4 pieces 1½˝ × 20½˝.

GRAY SOLID:

Cut 1 strip 1½˝ × WOF; subcut into 2 pieces 1½˝ × 20½˝.

Cut 1 strip 20½˝ × WOF; subcut into 2 pieces 20½˝ × 16½˝ for backing.

INSTRUCTIONS

All seam allowances are ¼˝.

Assembling the Pillow Top

1. Use 6 blue solid pieces measuring 1½˝ × 2½˝ and 9 print pieces to make 3 strips as shown, sewing along the 2½˝ sides. Press the seams toward the print fabric.

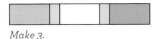

Make 3.

2. Use 8 blue solid pieces measuring 1½˝ × 4½˝ and 10 print pieces to make 2 strips as shown, sewing along the 4½˝ sides. Press the seams toward the print fabric.

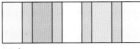

Make 2.

3. Arrange the strips into columns. Sew blue solid strips 1½˝ × 14½˝ between the columns. Then sew blue solid strips to the right and left. Press the seams toward the blue solid strips. Sew a 1½˝ × 20½˝ blue solid strip to the top and bottom.

4. Sew 1½˝ × 20½˝ gray strips at the top and bottom, and then sew another 1½˝ × 20½˝ blue solid strip to the top and bottom. Press. The pillow top should measure 20½˝ × 20½˝.

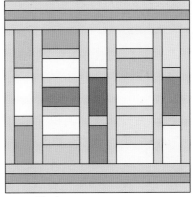

Assembly diagram

Quilting and Finishing

1. Mark quilting designs on the pillow top, or plan to quilt without marking.

2. Layer the muslin lining, batting, and pillow top; baste.

3. Quilt as desired by hand or machine. Trim all layers to 20½˝ × 20½˝.

4. Using your favorite closure method, add the backing. My materials and cutting instructions allow for a simple envelope-style backing—see Pillow Construction Techniques (page 116).

*Pillow*POP

GARDEN DISTRICT

Finished size: 19½˝ × 19½˝

The bright blossoms on this pillow top seem to be climbing a trellis of sashing strips. Hand stitching brings out the layered design, which is accentuated by the juxtaposition of straight lines and curves.

ARTIST: *Corey Yoder*
WEBSITE: littlemissshabby.com

Materials and Supplies

TAN SOLID: ¾ yard for background and binding

ASSORTED PRINTS: scraps totaling ½ yard

LIGHTWEIGHT INTERFACING: 18˝ × 30˝

BACKING: ½ yard

BATTING: 22˝ × 22˝

PILLOW FORM: 20˝ × 20˝

Cutting

TAN SOLID:

Cut 9 squares 6½˝ × 6½˝ for the background.

Cut 2 strips 1¼˝ × WOF; subcut into 6 pieces 1¼˝ × 6½˝ and 2 pieces 1¼˝ × 20˝ for the sashing.

Cut 2 strips 2½˝ × WOF for the binding.

ASSORTED PRINTS:

Cut strips of various colors 2½˝ long, ranging in width from 1˝ to 2¼˝.

Corey is a fabric-loving full-time mom with a passion for quilts and quilt design. A fourth-generation quilter, she has been surrounded by fabric and quilts her whole life. Corey's love of fabric led her to quilt making, followed by the opening of her children's clothing and appliqué business, Little Miss Shabby, and finally back to quilts and quilt design. Corey enjoys the challenge of precision-piecing traditional quilts and giving them a modern twist with current fabrics and new design elements. Her designs and published patterns often combine embroidery and appliqué, utilizing bright and fun fabrics.

INSTRUCTIONS

Use the Garden District petal template pattern (page 127).

All seam allowances are ¼″.

Assembling the Pillow Top

1. Sew print strips together to form 36 strip sets 2½″ × 6½″, or slightly longer than 6½″.

2. Use the petal template to trace and cut a petal shape from each strip set.

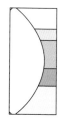

3. Use the same template to cut out 36 petal shapes from the interfacing.

4. Sew the interfacing petals to the right side of the fabric petals, sewing along the curved edge only, using a ¼″ seam allowance. Turn right side out, press, and trim away the interfacing, leaving about ¼″ of the interfacing turned under the curve.

5. Sew a petal unit to each side of each tan square by topstitching, sewing only along the curve. Trim away the tan background fabric under the petal, about ¼˝ from the curve.

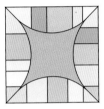

6. Sew 2 sashing strips 1¼˝ × 6½˝ between the 3 blocks of each row; sew the 1¼˝ × 20˝ sashing strips between the rows, as shown in the assembly diagram. The pillow top should measure 20˝ × 20˝.

Quilting and Finishing

1. Layer and baste the batting and pillow top. Quilt as desired—I used a decorative running stitch following the curves of each petal and going across the sashing, using variegated embroidery thread.

2. Refer to Pillow Construction Techniques (page 116) to make an envelope backing.

3. Pin the backing pieces to the pillow top, right sides facing out, overlapping the backing pieces. Baste ¼˝ from the edge.

4. Create the binding and attach it to the pillow as described in Double-Fold Straight-Grain Binding (page 119). Insert the pillow form.

Assembly diagram

PILLOW CONSTRUCTION TECHNIQUES

ENVELOPE BACKING

1. Cut 2 rectangles from backing fabric ½˝ longer than the finished pillow size and 3˝ wider than half the finished size, or as specified in the project.

2. Hem a long side of each rectangle: Turn under ½˝, press, turn under ½˝ again, and press. Topstitch ⅛˝ from the folded edge and again ¼˝ from the folded edge.

> **tip** *If you own a serger, use it to clean-finish the seams. If not, a tight zigzag will do the trick. Do not serge or zigzag over the straight stitches, or stitches may be visible when you turn the pillow right side out.*

3. Place a backing piece on the pillow top, right sides together, aligning raw edges, and pin. Sew with a ½˝ seam allowance, or use seam allowance specified for the project. Backstitch at the beginning and end. Trim seams at the corners.

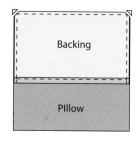

4. Place the second backing piece on the pillow top as shown, pin, and sew. The overlapping area in the middle will be reinforced because it gets sewn twice. Trim seams at the corners.

5. Turn right side out through the envelope opening, pushing out the corners. Insert a pillow form.

ENVELOPE BACKING WITH BINDING

1. Cut backing pieces as specified in the project, or use size guidelines from Step 1 of Envelope Backing (page 116).

2. For the decorative binding, cut a strip 2½˝ wide and 1˝ longer than the pillow size. Fold the strip in half lengthwise, wrong sides together, and press. Unfold, and press under ⅝˝ on each side so raw edges meet in the middle. Refold and press—all raw edges are concealed.

3. Sew binding to the long side of a backing piece, encasing the raw edge of the backing piece in the binding. This side of the backing will show on the pillow back. Trim the excess.

4. Continue as for Envelope Backing, Step 3; make sure you sew the bound side of the backing to the pillow top first, and then the plain hemmed side.

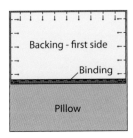

ENVELOPE BACKING WITH LINING

1. Cut backing fabric as specified in the project, or in Step 1 of Envelope Backing (page 116). Cut 2 pieces of muslin or other lining fabric the same size.

2. Right sides together, pin and sew each backing piece to a lining piece on a long side.

3. Turn right side out, press, and topstitch along the seamed edge.

4. Continue as for Envelope Backing, Step 3.

BUTTONED BACK CLOSURE

1. Cut the backing pieces as specified in the project, or see Step 1 of Envelope Backing (page 116). Hem the backing pieces as described in Step 2 of Envelope Backing. If you prefer a lined backing to support the buttonhole and button, follow the steps in Envelope Backing with Lining (above).

2. Measure the button. Mark the desired buttonholes on the hemmed side of a backing piece (or the finished side, if backing is lined.)

3. Sew buttonholes as marked, and cut open with a seam ripper or buttonhole tool.

4. Continue as for Envelope Backing, Step 3—make sure you sew the backing piece with the buttonholes to the pillow top first, then the other backing piece.

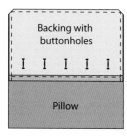

5. Mark the buttonhole location on the other backing piece, and sew on the buttons.

ZIPPER BACKING

1. Cut a piece of backing fabric the same width as the pillow top, but ½˝ longer. Turn under ½˝ along the width.

2. Using a zipper approximately 2˝ longer than the pillow top, pin the closed zipper, pull-side down, on the right side of the pillow top's bottom edge.

3. Sew zipper in place using a zipper foot, adjusting the needle position for a tight seam.

4. Slide the zipper pull past the pillow's edge to get it out of the way. Press, and topstitch.

5. Close the zipper. Pin the folded edge of the backing fabric on the zipper. Sew in place, press, and topstitch.

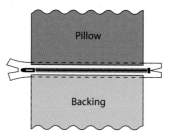

6. Unzip the zipper halfway. *Do not* leave it zipped completely—you need to turn the pillow right side out later.

7. Pin the pillow top and backing right sides together. Using a standard sewing foot, start at a corner and sew a ½˝ seam (or as specified in the project) around the pillow. Backstitch multiple times over the zipper corners to anchor the zipper.

8. Trim the excess zipper length. Snip the seam allowances of the non-zippered pillow corners at a 45° angle. Turn right side out and press.

DOUBLE-FOLD STRAIGHT-GRAIN BINDING

Trim the batting and backing even with the edges of the pillow top.

1. For a ¼˝ finished binding, cut binding strips 2˝ wide, or use the width specified in the project. Place a strip right side facing up and place another strip at 90°, right sides together. Sew as shown. Trim the seam allowances to ¼˝ and press open.

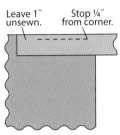

Step 1

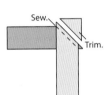

Sew.
Trim.

Sew diagonal seam.

Press diagonal seam open.

2. Press the entire strip in half lengthwise with wrong sides together. With raw edges even, pin binding to the pillow top a few inches away from a corner, leaving the first few inches of binding unattached. Check the project instructions—you may need to attach the binding to the back rather than the front. Sew using a ¼˝ seam allowance.

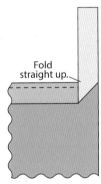

Step 2

3. Stop sewing ¼˝ from the first corner (see Step 1) and back-stitch a stitch. Lift the presser foot and needle, and rotate the pillow top a quarter turn. Fold the binding at a right angle so it extends straight above the pillow and the fold forms a 45° angle in the corner (see Step 2); then bring it down even with the edge of the pillow (see Step 3). Begin sewing at the folded edge. Repeat at all corners.

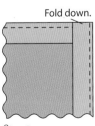

Step 3

4. Continue stitching until you are back near the beginning of the binding strip. Fold under the beginning tail of the binding strip ¼˝ so the raw edge is turned under. Tuck the end tail into the folded beginning. Continue to sew the binding slightly beyond the starting stitches. Trim the excess. Fold the binding over the raw edges to the pillow back and hand stitch, mitering the corners.

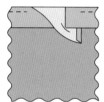

HALF-SQUARE TRIANGLES

Refer to the project instructions for the size of the squares.

1. With right sides together, pair 2 squares. Lightly draw a diagonal line from a corner to the opposite corner on the wrong side of a square.

2. Stitch a scant ¼˝ on each side of the drawn line.

3. Cut on the line. Each pair of squares will make 2 half-square triangles.

4. Press the seam, either pressing toward the darker fabric or pressing open. Be careful to avoid stretching.

5. Trim the dog-ears—the triangles sticking out at the ends.

FLYING GEESE

Refer to the project instructions for the size of the squares and rectangle.

1. Lightly draw a diagonal line from a corner to the opposite corner on the wrong sides of 2 squares.

2. With right sides together, place a square on an end of the rectangle. Sew directly on the line, trim the seam allowance to ¼˝, and press open.

3. With right sides together, place the other square on the other end of the rectangle. Sew directly on the line, trim the seam allowance to ¼˝, and press open.

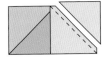 

TEMPLATES

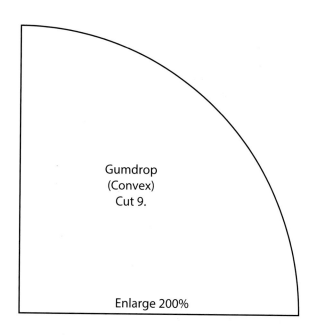

Gumdrop
(Convex)
Cut 9.

Enlarge 200%

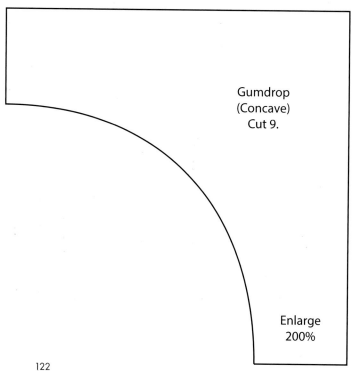

Gumdrop
(Concave)
Cut 9.

Enlarge
200%

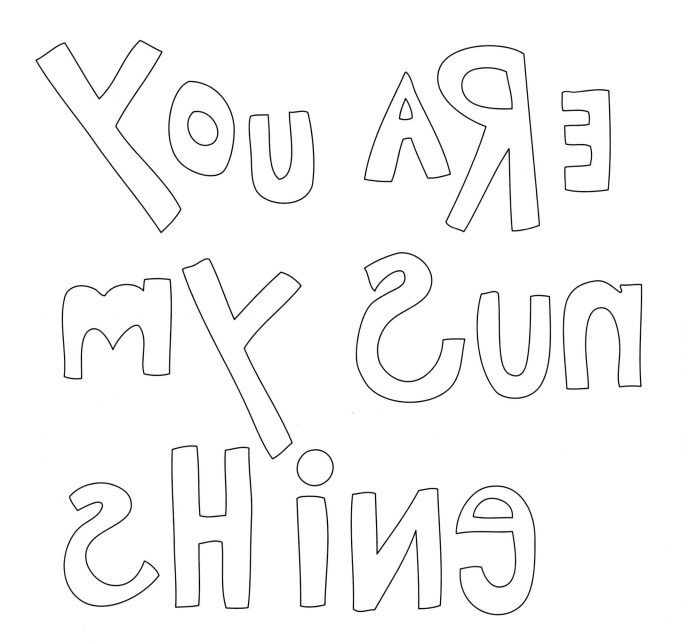

123

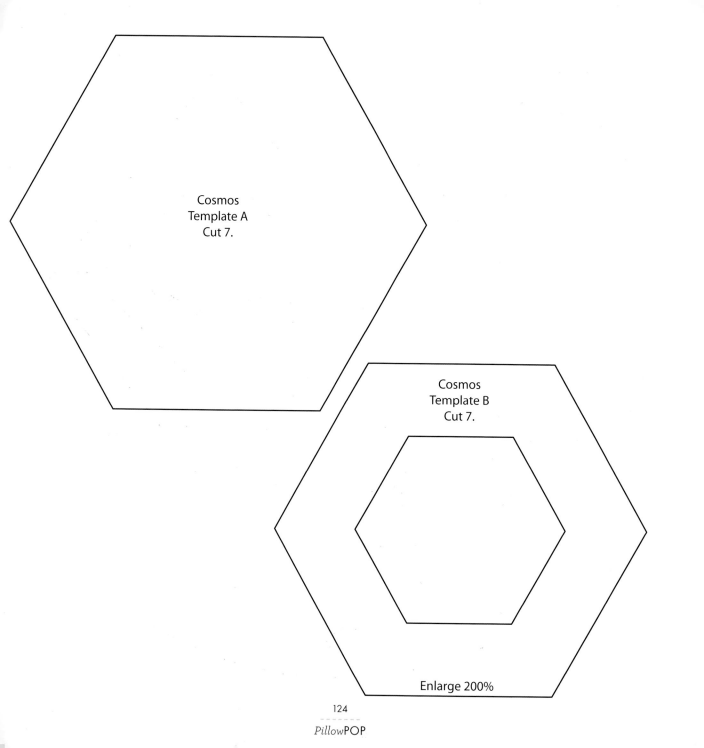

Cosmos
Template A
Cut 7.

Cosmos
Template B
Cut 7.

Enlarge 200%

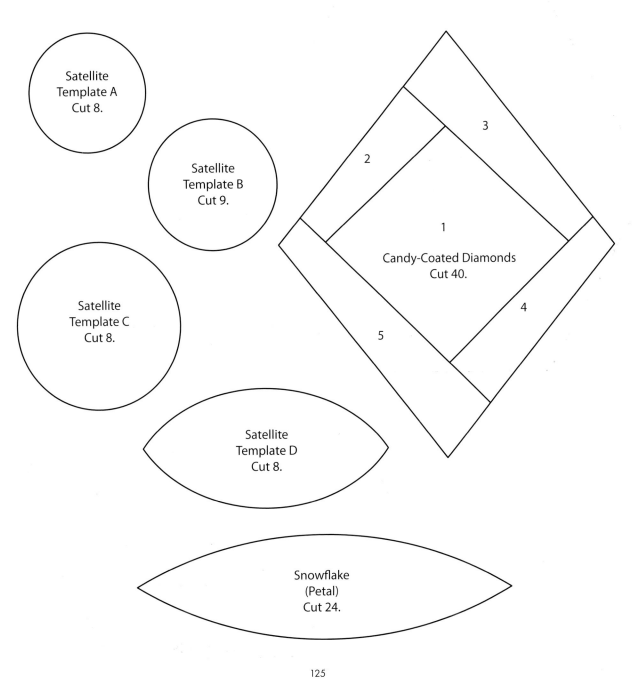

Satellite
Template A
Cut 8.

Satellite
Template B
Cut 9.

Satellite
Template C
Cut 8.

Satellite
Template D
Cut 8.

Candy-Coated Diamonds
Cut 40.

1

2

3

4

5

Snowflake
(Petal)
Cut 24.

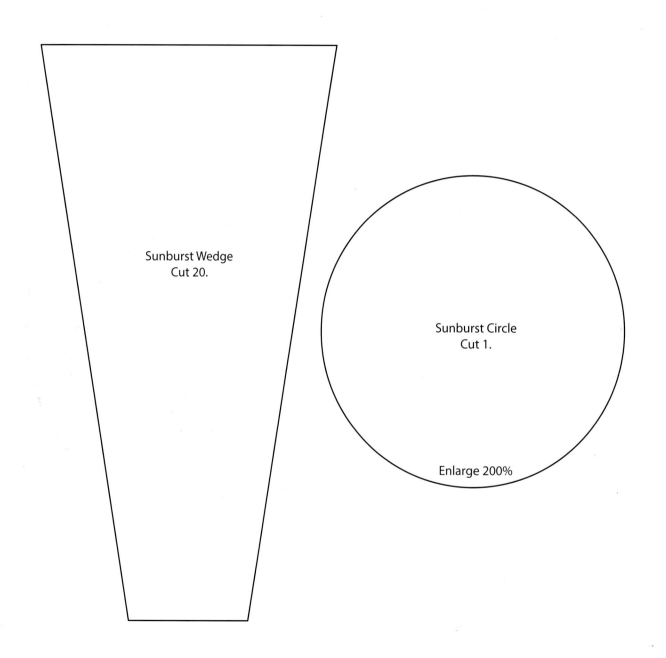

Sunburst Wedge
Cut 20.

Sunburst Circle
Cut 1.

Enlarge 200%

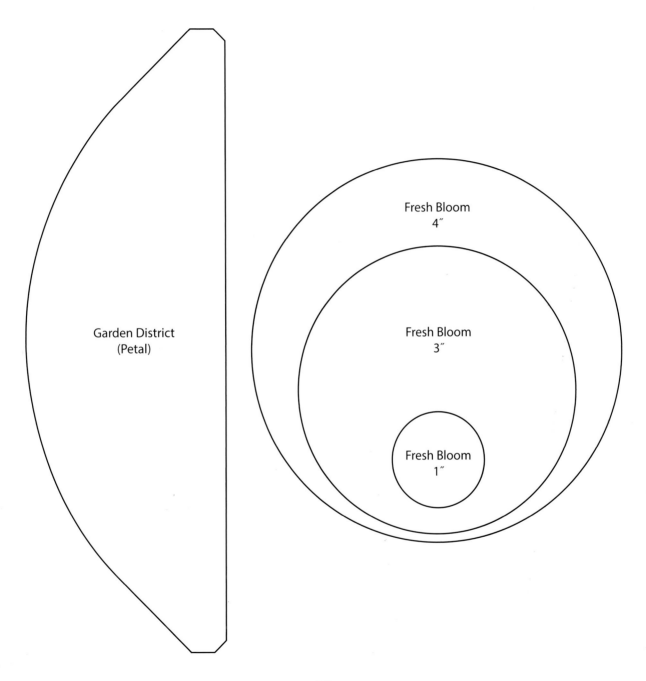

Garden District
(Petal)

Fresh Bloom
4″

Fresh Bloom
3″

Fresh Bloom
1″

stashBOOKS

fabric arts for a handmade lifestyle

If you're craving beautiful authenticity in a time of mass-production...Stash Books is for you. Stash Books is a line of how-to books celebrating fabric arts for a handmade lifestyle. Backed by C&T Publishing's solid reputation for quality, Stash Books will inspire you with contemporary designs, clear and simple instructions, and engaging photography.

www.stashbooks.com